PUBLIC RECORD OFFICE READERS' GUIDE No 15

PREROGATIVE COURT OF CANTERBURY

WILLS
AND
OTHER PROBATE
RECORDS

Miriam Scott

PRO Publications

929.3

PRO Publications
Public Record Office
Ruskin Avenue
Kew
Surrey
TW9 4DU

Contents

Illustrations

Using the Public Record Office

The Public Record Office (PRO) is at Kew where original records are held.

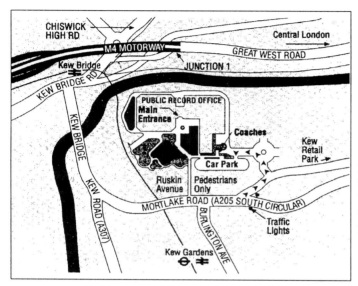

**Public Record Office,
Ruskin Avenue, Kew,
Surrey TW9 4DU.**
The telephone number is:
0181-876-3444.

Hours of opening
From 7 April 1997

Monday	9.30 am to 5.00 pm
Tuesday	10.00 am to 7.00 pm
Wednesday	9.30 am to 5.00 pm
Thursday	9.00 am to 7.00 pm
Friday	9.30 am to 5.00 pm

and from 5 July 1997

Saturday	9.00 am to 5.00 pm

Certain popular classes are viewed on microfilm, and some can be seen at the Office's central London microfilm reading room which is at:

**Family Records Centre
Myddelton Street,
London
EC1 1UW.**
The telephone number is:
0181-392-5300.

Hours of opening
From 10 March 1997

Monday	9.00 am to 5.00 pm
Tuesday	10.00 am to 7.00 pm
Wednesday	9.00 am to 5.00 pm
Thursday	9.00 am to 7.00 pm
Friday	9.00 am to 5.00 pm
Saturday	9.30 am to 5.00 pm

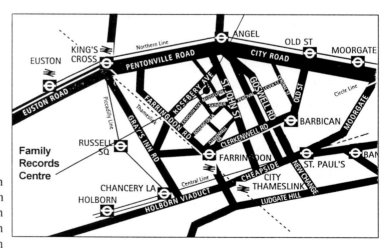

The office at Kew is closed on public holidays and for annual stocktaking (usually the first two weeks in October), but the central London reading room will not close for stocktaking.

When you first visit the PRO, please bring with you formal documentary proof of identity bearing your name and signature. If you are not a British citizen you will need to bring your passport or national identity card. You will then be issued with a Reader's Ticket. Without a valid ticket you cannot be admitted to the reading rooms or order documents. You do not need one to visit the central London microfilm reading room.

You may use only graphite pencils in the reading rooms. Pens of any kind are not allowed. You may use personal computers, typewriters and tape recorders in designated areas. A full list of Reading Room rules is available on request.

Each document has a unique three-part reference. The first part is the lettercode, for example PROB for the records of the Prerogative Court of Canterbury or IR for Inland Revenue, according to the provenance of the documents, but with the growth of bureaucracy the letters given do not necessarily bear any resemblance to the body concerned, eg Council on Tribunals is BL. The second part is the class number, which represents the series within the lettercode. The third part is the piece number, which represents the individual document.

To identify the lettercode and class, consult the published Current Guide, which is the primary guide to the holdings of the PRO. The Current Guide is in three parts. Part 1 describes the history and functions of government departments. Part 2 briefly describes each class with information such as the covering dates and number of pieces. Part 3 is the index to the other two parts. There is no general detailed index covering records in the PRO. Once possible classes have been identified, the next step is to consult the class lists which briefly describe each piece. These are available in the PRO reading or reference rooms.

Records held on microfilm by the central London reading room are as follows:

PROB 6	Prerogative Court of Canterbury Administrations 1796-1857
PROB 11	Prerogative Court of Canterbury registered copy wills 1384-1858
IR 26	Death Duty records 1796-1857
IR 27	Death Duty indexes 1858-1903
RG 4	Non parochial Registers, registers of births, marriages and deaths 1567-1858
HO 107	1841-1851 Census returns
RG 9-RG 12	1861-1891 Census returns

Acknowledgements

I am grateful to the many friends and colleagues who read the text in typescript and made useful comments on it. These include: Bill Elton-Craig who has never been to the PRO and had never heard of the PCC; Anne Clinch, a family historian with knowledge of other probate records, but not of the PCC; and Anthony Attwood, Elizabeth Hull and Bill Keymer, checkers of the Friends' PROB 12 project, who know the PCC pretty well!

I am also grateful to all the volunteers who worked so hard on the project, notably Keith Fairclough; and in particular to Eileen Startin for giving me the idea for the alphabet in appendix E, and to Bob Orme for producing the first graph of distribution by county which led to the one in appendix A.

I am indebted to the Guildhall Library for supplying the correct references to the House of Commons Sessional Papers; to Mary Kift for allowing me to use the material in chapter 7; to Elizabeth Hull for the examples of a nuncupative will and limited administration in chapter 2; to Hilary Marshall for commenting on the presentation of the family tree; and to Anthony Camp for reading the chapter on the eighteenth century indexes and suggesting a useful addition to it. I have appreciated the encouragement given me by Alfred Knightbridge and his meticulous work in correcting the proofs.

I shall always be grateful for the kindness and courtesy of members of the PRO staff which made my time as compiler of the Dorset index and organiser of the Friends' project so congenial. Above all I am indebted to Gervase Hood for the generosity with which he has shared with me his unrivalled knowledge of the PCC.

None of this would have been possible without the computer programs created by my son William (Bill Scott) or the constant help and support of my husband, Donald.

Foreword

The book is intended primarily for beginners, but readers already familiar with the records of the Prerogative Court of Canterbury (PCC) in PROB 11 and PROB 6 may find some chapters which will encourage them to explore classes hitherto unknown to them. The appendixes, too, may prove useful to them for reference in the reading room.

Since most readers start with the nineteenth century, that is where this guide starts. Most researchers work backwards chronologically: so does this guide, hoping to give them at the beginning what they need to know in order to get started. References in the text to 'working backwards' refer to this process of working backwards chronologically in the process of biographical research.

Nineteenth-century wills and administrations are the most difficult to find these days, there being almost no modern indexes after 1800, and so the chapter explaining how to do this is the longest. It is hoped that by the time readers have progressed to the earlier periods they will have gained sufficient expertise and the confidence to ask for help if they need it.

In direct quotations from the PCC records I have sometimes added a little punctuation, where I thought this helpful.

Readers will notice that many of my examples are from Dorset. This is not because Dorset is represented more than other counties in the records of the PCC (one glance at the graph in appendix A will correct any such impression) but because I came across them when compiling the second edition of *An Index to Dorset PCC Wills and Administrations 1821-1858*. And I started this index for the very good reason that most of my ancestors lived in Dorset!

The guide has been written to be up to date in March 1997. All the information applies to the new situation after the closure of Chancery Lane when original documents will be available only at Kew. However, certain classes which have been microfilmed will then be available in the PRO's new central London reading room as well as at Kew.

Introduction

Readers already familiar with probate records other than those of the Prerogative Court of Canterbury (PCC) may go straight to Chapter 1 on page 1.

Wills and administrations for the whole of England and Wales after 11 January 1858 are held by the Principal Registry of the Family Division of the High Court of Justice, at present in Somerset House. Any references in this book to 'the nineteenth-century' therefore refer only to the years 1800-1858.

Until 1858 there were many different courts in England and Wales which had the right to prove wills and give grants of administration and most of these were church courts. The Prerogative Court of Canterbury (PCC) was the most important of these courts and its records are held by the Public Record Office (PRO). Wills proved by other courts are usually held in county record offices and other archive repositories. Details can be found in the Federation of Family History Societies' booklet *Probate Jurisdictions: where to look for wills*, and the areas served by the various local courts are also shown on the parish maps of individual counties published by the Institute of Heraldic and Genealogical Studies (IHGS). Details of these publications are given in the bibliography.

In theory, if you had personal property (or *personalty*, see glossary) in only one archdeaconry, your will could be proved in the archdeacon's court. If you had personal property in more than one archdeaconry, but all in one diocese, your will could be proved in the bishop's court, usually known as the consistory court. If you had personal property in more than one diocese your will could be proved in the prerogative court of one of the archbishops: if it was all in the province of Canterbury (see map in appendix A) then in the PCC, but if in the province of York then in the Prerogative Court of York. However, if your personal property was in more than one ecclesiastical province then it would be proved in both the PCC and the Prerogative Court of York. In such instances the probate grant would be limited to the property in that particular province.

There were, however, rules about which wills could be proved in the PCC but they were not always observed in practice. In theory your will could be proved in the PCC if you had personal property in more than one diocese of the ecclesiastical province of Canterbury and that property was worth more than £5 (£10 in the dioceses of London and Lincoln). If you see a reference to the deceased having property 'sufficient to found the jurisdiction of the Prerogative Court of Canterbury' (such as that shown in the Latin grant of administration on page 22) it is referring to this qualification.

But even by the eighteenth century this qualification was merely notional and the status of the PCC and its reputation for safekeeping of the records resulted in many other wills being proved there. Numbers increased still further from 1819 when a legal ruling resulted in the wills of the great majority of people holding Bank of England stock being proved in the PCC.

If someone died intestate, that is, without leaving a valid will, the court could make a grant of Administration (often abbreviated to Admon.) to the next-of-kin, principal creditor or any other person who could claim a legitimate interest in the personal estate. These grants are recorded in the administration act books.

From 1796 a possible guide to where a will was proved or an administration granted is provided by the death duty indexes. Full treatment of this subject is beyond the scope of this book, but a short note showing how to use the death duty registers to discover in which court a will was proved will be found in chapter 8.

However, not all estates were subject to death duty, so when all else fails I have sometimes suggested as a rough rule-of-thumb that the PCC should be the second place you look for a will or administration, having first searched in the records of the appropriate local courts.

1. The Nineteenth Century 1801-1858

If you already have a reference for a will or administration (for example, from a printed index you have consulted in a library) omit the section on indexes and go straight to **1.1.3 Using the reference: Wills**.

1.1 PROB 12: Indexes of wills and administrations 1801-1858

With a few exceptions, there are no modern indexes for the period 1801-1852. You will have to consult the copies of the 'calendars' in the class PROB 12. These are indexed under initial letter only, in annual calendars, and in roughly chronological order within the one letter. Thus if you are looking for the will of someone whose surname begins with B, you will have to look through all the Bs of the year you consider most likely. It will help if you know the date of death. For example, if your ancestor died in September 1832, you can select the volume for 1832, turn to the section for the letter B, and then turn straight to the page where the September wills begin, search to the end of the year, and then do the same for the administrations. If necessary, continue the search through several more years. Grants were often made several years after the person's death, especially if there was any dispute.

For the period 1853 to January 1858 there is a fully alphabetical printed index. This is also available in some libraries and record offices which are listed on page 12 of the Federation of Family History Societies (FFHS) booklet *Probate Jurisdictions: where to look for wills* (see bibliography).

During part of the nineteenth century the names of non-commissioned soldiers and sailors, including those of the East India Company and merchant seamen, were listed separately in the calendars in PROB 12. From 1800 to 1819 they appear at the end of the section for each letter. From 1820 to 1852 they are all in a separate section at the end of the volume. (A page from the list for 1837 is reproduced as page 19.) But in the printed indexes from 1853 to 1858 they are included in the main alphabetical sequence.

Commissioned officers, however, were always listed in the main sequence of names, as you can see from the example on page 14.

Note that a bishop was usually listed under the name of his diocese, not under his surname. Bishops did not retire in those days!

1.1.1 Understanding the reference

An example of a page of PROB 12 is reproduced on page 4. Each entry is given in the order - surname, forename, place of residence, month of grant, and, for wills, a number which is a quire number (see 1.2.1). In some cases there is extra information, and this is dealt with in section 4 of this chapter.

1.1.2 Place of residence

The meaning of the entry in this column is usually quite clear, and normally relates to the county. Note that Southton is an abbreviation for Southamptonshire, the old name for Hampshire and Northton is Northamptonshire. North Britain is Scotland. If you find the name of a county town, bear in mind the possibility that it may indicate the whole county. Chester means the county of Cheshire, not just the town of Chester, and Ely the Isle of Ely, etc., but Bristol, Coventry, Exeter, Norwich and Salisbury (or Sarum) do indicate the towns.

Pts is the abbreviation for the Latin phrase *in partibus transmarinis* (in countries overseas) and is used for people who died abroad or at sea.

	Reference			PROB 11
This Margin **not to be** **used.**	PROB 11	Date	Quire Numbers	Volume Number
	1961	1842	251 - 300	6
	1962	1842	301 - 350	7
	1963	1842	351 - 400	8
	1964	1842	401 - 450	9
	1965	1842	451 - 500	10
	1966	1842	501 - 550	11
	1967	1842	551 - 600	12
	1968	1842	601 - 650	13
	1969	1842	651 - 700	14
	1970	1842	701 - 750	15
	1971	1842	751 - 800	16
	1972	1842	801 - 865	17
	1973	1843	1 - 50	1
	1974	1843	51 - 100	2
	1975	1843	101 - 150	3
	1976	1843	151 - 200	4
	1977	1843	201 - 250	5
	1978	1843	251 - 300	6
	1979	1843	301 - 350	7
	1980	1843	351 - 400	8
	1981	1843	401 - 450	9
	1982	1843	451 - 500	10
	1983	1843	501 - 550	11
	1984	1843	551 - 600	12
	1985	1843	601 - 650	13
	1986	1843	651 - 700	14
	1987	1843	701 - 750	15
	1988	1843	751 - 800	16
	1989	1843	801 - 850	17
	1990	1843	851 - 900	18

Fig 1   A page from the PROB 11 class list.

Wills 1842

	Stewart	Elizabeth	Surrey	Apl 293
	Steer	William	Surrey	Apl 293
	Silvester	Maria	Oxford	Apl 293
	Shenton	James)		
		Richard)	Leicester	Apl 293
	Smith	Mary	Essex	Apl 293
	Siminton	Mary)		
		Elizabeth)	Middx	Apl 293
	Symmons	Richard	Dorset	Apl 293
	Seward	Francis	Devon	Apl 293
Esqre	Sherfield	James	Oxford	Apl 293
Esqre	Sherson	Robert	Middx	Apl 293
	Sims	Eliza		
		Catherine	York	Apl 293
	Spiller	Robert	Devon	Apl 293
	Salter	Elizabeth	Stafford	Apl 293
	Swinton	George		
		Alexander	Cambridge	Apl 293
	Shirley	Elizabeth	Kent	Apl 294
	Stowell	William		
		Stow	Durham	Apl 294
Esqre	Seton	George	North Brits	Apl 294
	Spooner	Betty	Somerset	Apl 294
	Syms	John	Middx	Apl 294
	Swale	Thomas)		
		Steele)	York	Apl 294
	Sharpe	William	Kent	Apl 294
Esqre	Smith	William	Hereford	Apl 294

Fig 2   A page from the PROB 12 calendar for 1842, showing references to wills.
PROB 12/251.

1.1.3 Using the reference: Wills

If you have been successful, you will now have a reference consisting of surname, forename, place of residence, month, and a number. The number is known as a quire number and refers to a series of sixteen pages in the register copies of wills in PROB 11. Several wills may therefore have the same quire number.

A page of PROB 12 is reproduced opposite showing the references for some of the wills proved in 1842. Suppose you wish to read the will of Elizabeth Stewart who lived in Surrey. Her will was proved in April and the quire number is 293. Make a note of the year as well as the full reference and turn to one of the volumes on the shelves, labelled PROB 11. This is the PROB 11 class list. Turn to the page which shows the piece numbers for 1842, and then look for the piece which includes the quire 293. This page is reproduced as page 3. Here you can see that the piece number for quires 251-300 is PROB 11/1961 (ignore the volume number). You can now help yourself to the microfilm containing PROB 11/1961.

> WARNING: Note that these four-figure piece numbers can look very much like dates especially around 1834 when the dates actually coincide with the piece numbers! You should therefore always make sure that in your notes you distinguish them, for example by putting a / immediately in front of the PROB 11 reference, even if you do not always repeat PROB 11. Otherwise you may become hopelessly confused!

PROB 11 is seen on microfilm. This saves wear and tear on the original documents and in this case has the advantage of making extremely heavy and unwieldy volumes more accessible to readers. It also means that they can be read in the PRO's central London reading room as well as at Kew.

1.2 PROB 11: Registers of copies of wills

1.2.1 Finding your place on the microfilm

First you need to find the right quire. Quire numbers are written in large figures at the top right hand (RH) corner on the first page only of the quire. At this stage ignore the small stamped numbers on every alternate page: these are folio numbers. The frames show right and left hand pages alternately so you will find eight RH pages in each quire, only the first of which will show the quire number. Make sure you are using an appropriate magnification for this search - one that shows a whole page at a time.

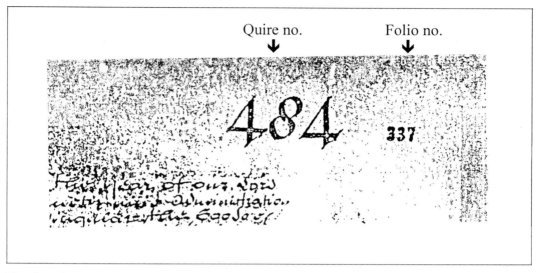

Having found the quire, look down the outside margin of each page until you come to the name of the person whose will you are looking for. You should now be able to read the will. You may like to change to a stronger magnification for difficult passages.

1.2.2 Reading the script

The script in which the wills are written in PROB 11 may be unfamiliar to you, but you will soon get used to it. Reference to the alphabet given as appendix E of this book may help you, especially with the capital letters, for example when deciphering the name of a parish. Many of your difficulties will be solved once you have realized that what looks like a small r is in fact a small c.

The similarity of the small n and small u is less of a problem to those looking for a particular name, and when reading words in context, than it is to indexers, but you do need to remember that the capital letters I and J were treated as one letter and therefore surnames beginning with these letters are mixed up together (in PROB 11 and the act books as well as in PROB 12). See the example reproduced on page 27.

Since you will be reading from film or photocopy you should note that when you see a single straight down-stroke this is probably not an l, which was always written with a loop, or leaning forward, but a t from which the side-stroke, made with the thin edge of the pen, has got lost in the filming.

If you would like a photocopy make a note of the frames you require on one of the forms provided (for this you will use the folio numbers). Full instructions are given on the back of the form.

Here are some commonly occurring words containing the small c. Note also that the loop of the h leans forward and that the e has no cross-bar!

executors	executors	*each*	each
Archibald	Archibald	*such*	such
which	which	*execution*	execution
acts	acts (not arts)	*concerning*	concerning
receipt	receipt	*declared*	declared

1.2.3 Administration (with the will annexed)

In PROB 12 you will sometimes find the terms *Admon Will* or *Ad Will*. These are abbreviations for *Administration (with the will annexed)*. Do not be misled by the term *administration*. These entries appear in the lists of wills in PROB 12 and the wills concerned are to be found in PROB 11 in the usual way.

The term was used when there was no surviving executor, or no executor able or willing to administer the estate, and a grant was made to another person to administer the estate in accordance with the will. The will of Betty Smith which is given in chapter 5 is a case where such a grant was made.

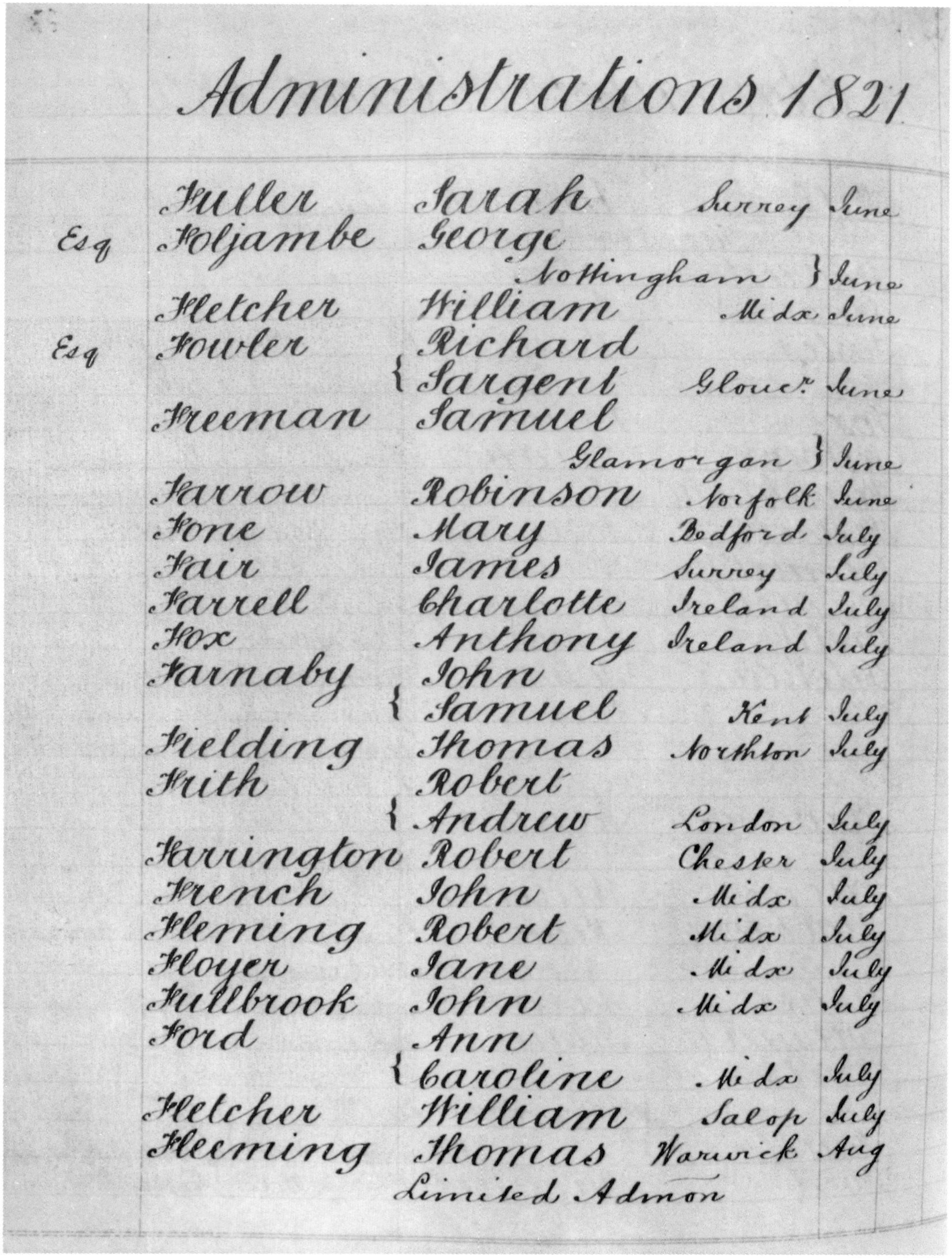

Administrations 1821

	Fuller	Sarah	Surrey	June
Esq	Foljambe	George	Nottingham	June
	Fletcher	William	Midx	June
Esq	Fowler	Richard { Sargent	Glouc.r	June
	Freeman	Samuel	Glamorgan	June
	Farrow	Robinson	Norfolk	June
	Fone	Mary	Bedford	July
	Fair	James	Surrey	July
	Farrell	Charlotte	Ireland	July
	Fox	Anthony	Ireland	July
	Farnaby	John { Samuel	Kent	July
	Fielding	Thomas	Northton	July
	Frith	Robert { Andrew	London	July
	Farrington	Robert	Chester	July
	French	John	Midx	July
	Fleming	Robert	Midx	July
	Floyer	Jane	Midx	July
	Fullbrook	John	Midx	July
	Ford	Ann { Caroline	Midx	July
	Fletcher	William	Salop	July
	Fleeming	Thomas	Warwick	Aug
		Limited Admon		

Fig 3 A page from the PROB 12 calendar for 1821, showing references to administrations. PROB 12/212

1.3 PROB 6: Administrations (Admons)

To find an administration you need to read one of the administration act books in PROB 6 which, like the registered wills in PROB 11, are available on microfilm and can be read in the central London reading room as well as at Kew.

In order to use PROB 6 you need to understand the arrangement of the act books. This information will also be useful to you if you should have occasion to consult any of the act books in PROB 7, PROB 8 or PROB 9.

1.3.1 The arrangement of the act books

From 1719, with some exceptions, the place of residence of the deceased governed the 'seat' which dealt with the administration of the estate and this arrangement continued until 1858. In the nineteenth century the act books are arranged in sections according to these 'seats' and in monthly sections within the seats. For easy reference the full list of the areas administered by each seat is given in appendix A. There you will also find a list of those cases where the grant was made in the Registrar's seat.

However, with the exception of the Registrar, it is not the name of the seat but the name of the clerk of the seat which is given at the beginning of each section of the act books! The PROB 6 finding-aid (on the shelves) will give you the information you need. A page is reproduced as page 10. This is the page you would use if you were looking for the administration of one of the entries on the page of 1821 administrations reproduced opposite. For example, to find the administration of Sarah Fuller (the first entry), take the film containing PROB 6/197, and turn to folio 61, where you will find a section headed 'Capes'. At that date Capes was the name of the clerk of the Surrey seat which dealt with all the counties south-west of London (see appendix A).

You will see that at this date there is only one act book (or piece) for each year in PROB 6. When you have taken your film, first make sure you have turned to the right piece number as there is sometimes more than one piece on a film - the piece number is given on every frame.

There are no quire numbers in the act books, but PROB 6 has folio numbers, on every alternate page.

At folio 61 Capes's section begins with January. But Sarah Fuller's administration was granted in June, so you can wind the film on to about half-way through this

County Seat	Clerk's Name	Folio Number
1820 PROB 6/196		
1 Registrar		1-67
2 Surrey	Capes	68-124
3 Welsh	Moore	126-161
4 Middx	Askew & Abbot	162-220
5 London	Moore	221-End
1821 PROB 6/197		
1 Registrar		1-60
2 Surrey	Capes	61-119
3 Welsh	Moore	120-160
4 Middx	Askew & Abbot	161-215
5 London	Moore	216-End
1822 PROB 6/198		
1 Registrar		1-78
2 Surrey	Capes	79-142
3 Wales	Moore	143-179
4 Middx	Askew & Abbot	181-243
5 London	Moore	244-End
1823 PROB 6/199		
1 Registrar		1-78
2 Surrey	Capes	79-139
3 Welsh	Moore	140-175
4 Middx	Askew & Abbot	176-251
5 London	Moore	253-End
1824 PROB 6/200		
1 Registrar		1-69
2 Surrey	Capes	70-130
3 Welsh	Moore	132-168
4 Middx	Askew & Abbot	169-239
5 London	Moore	241-End

Fig 4   A page from the PROB 6 finding aid.

section to find the page headed June. Ask for help if necessary.

Do not rely on the apparent alphabetical order of the surnames within the months. There are often additional entries at the end of the monthly section. It is worth searching the whole section if you cannot find what you want immediately. Remember that some Middlesex parishes were subject to the London seat and that 'London' meant only the City of London. The West End and much of the area north of the river Thames, which we think of as London today, was in Middlesex.

After all this trouble you may be disappointed with what you find. The grant of administration may tell you very little. Here is a typical example:

> Nancy Fisher On the fourth day Admon of the Goods Chattels and Credits of Nancy Fisher late of Milnthorpe in the County of Westmorland Widow deceased was granted to Robert Fisher one of the natural and lawful Children having been first sworn duly to administer.

The page of PROB 6/216 on which this administration appears is reproduced overleaf. The grant appears in the Registrar's seat because Westmorland was not in the province of Canterbury (see appendix A).

Another page from the Registrar's seat illustrates various cases when administrations were granted in this seat. Of the entries on page 13, Robert Viner Ellis died at sea, Mary Elliott's administration was granted by interlocutory decree, Jacques Gastambide and Elizabeth Gedney lived abroad, and Alexander Gerard lived in Scotland. For interlocutory decrees see chapter 6.1. As you can see from these examples, you may be lucky and gain extra information from an administration.

From 1796, as a result of the imposition of taxes commonly known as death duties, a rough valuation of the estate appears in the left hand margin under the name. It was often subsequently amended.

> Note: The numbers given in PROB 12 for administrations in the years 1843 (from the letter C) to 1846, which look like quire numbers, are in fact folio numbers. They refer to the original hand-written numbers, and not the stamped ones. It is easy to find administrations in these years!

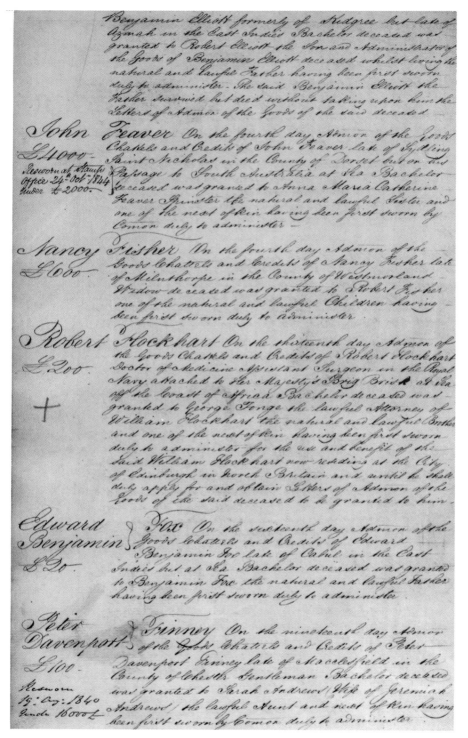

Fig 5 A page from an administration act book, June 1840. PROB 6/216, f 32 LH.

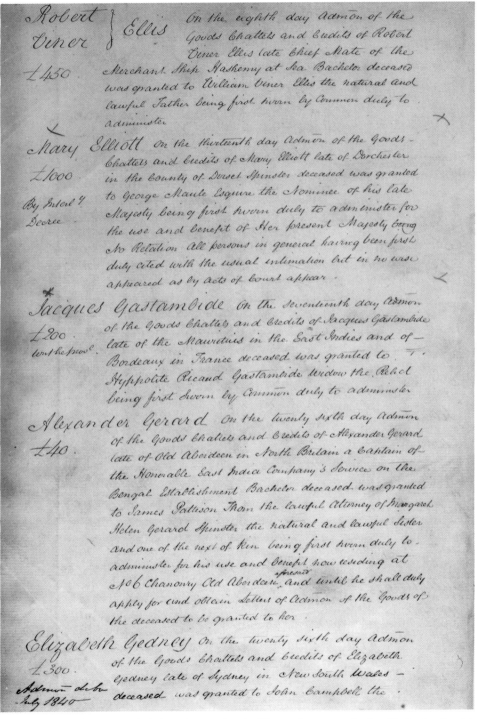

Fig 6   A page from an administration act book, illustrating cases dealt with in the Registrar's seat, Feb 1840. PROB 6/216, f 8 LH.

1.4 A little more on PROB 12

For some of the entries in PROB 12 a little more information is given. Sometimes it is about the occupation or status of the deceased. Examples from the PROB 12 volume for 1825 are shown here:

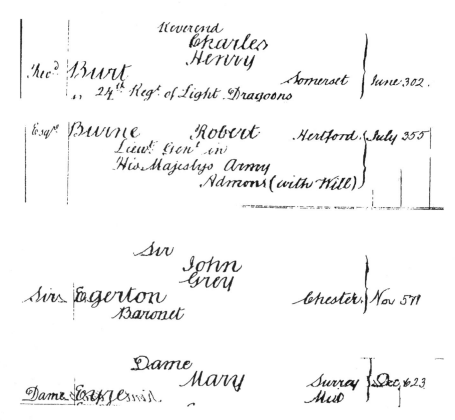

Otherwise it is information about the kind of grant. Where there is a further grant of probate on a will which had been proved earlier or on an administration, you will be given the information you need to find the will or first grant.

You will sometimes see a former surname given for women. Do not assume that this is a maiden name: it is often a name from a previous marriage.

1.4.1 References to earlier grants of probate

Here is an entry in the PROB 12 volume for 1825:

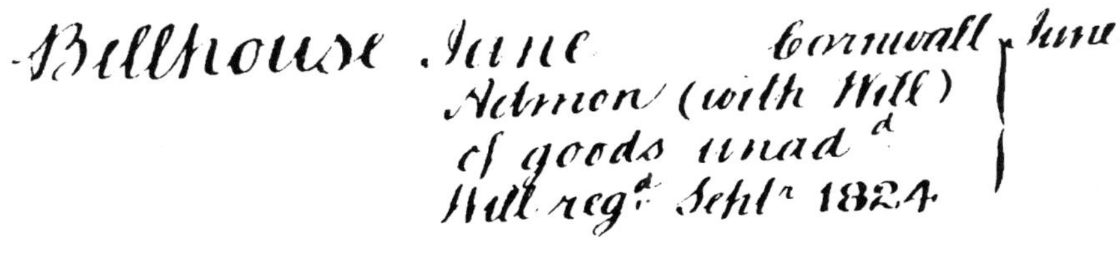
Bellhouse Jane Cornwall June
Admon (with Will)
of goods unad^d
Will reg^d Septr 1824

You will notice that in the entry for Jane Bellhouse there is no quire number. This is because the will is not in the PROB 11 register for 1825 but in that for 1824. To find the quire number turn to the PROB 12 volume for 1824, find the B pages for wills, then September, and there you will find the reference you need:

Bellhouse Jane Cornwall Sep 503

A note of the later grant will usually appear as a marginal note added near the end of the will in PROB 11, as it does here. If not, you will find the details in the probate act book in PROB 8 (see chapter 4). In this case, the sole executrix died before she had finished dealing with her sister's estate and so a further grant had to be made.

On the 23d June 1825 Adm[inistrati]on with the Will ann[exe]d, of the Goods Chattels and Credits of Jane Bellhouse late of Falmouth in the County of Cornwall Widow deceased left unadministered by Philippa Hull Widow dec[ease]d, whilst living the Sister sole Executrix and Residuary Legatee named in the said will, was granted to Elizabeth Jane Hull Sp[inste]r the Daughter and Administratrix of the goods of the said Philippa Hull Widow dec[ease]d having been first sworn by Commission duly to Administer.

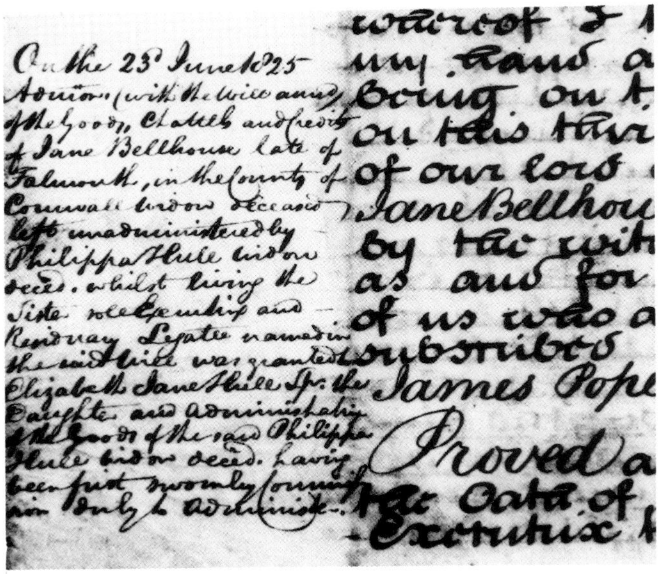

Fig 7 An example of a subsequent grant of probate entered in the will register. PROB 11/1690 quire 503.

But here is a different kind of reference to an earlier will taken from the PROB 12 volume for 1825:

*Fortune   Theodosia Monmouth May
Admon (with Will)
of goods unad.
Will regd. 825. Marriott*

Until 1840, the will register for each year was given a name, often the name of a prominent person whose will was contained in it. For example, the register for the year 1734 is called Ockham, after Lord King of Ockham, the Exeter grocer's son who became Lord Chancellor and was responsible for the act ordering English to be used in legal documents instead of Latin. A complete alphabetical list of these registers and their corresponding years is given as appendix C and can also be found at the end of the PROB 11 class list. In the case illustrated here the reference is to the register Marriott, which is the register for 1803. Here you are given the quire number so you can go straight to the PROB 11 class list to find the piece number and the film you need.

These subsequent grants are often a useful pointer to the date of death of a beneficiary, and you may find you have been taken back an extra generation or two since some subsequent grants refer to wills proved as many as seventy-five years earlier.

Beware of names of will registers which look like names of places. This example is taken from the PROB 12 volume for 1821:

*Astley   Philip   Surrey | Dec.
Double Probate
Will regd. 592 Bridport*

Here, Bridport is not a place of residence but the name of the register for 1814. Philip Astley lived in Surrey.

1.4.2 References to earlier administrations

*Kingsmill John   Pt Feb
Admon of goods
unad. Former grant
October 1822*

16

This example from the PROB 12 volume for 1825 shows that the original administration was granted in October 1822. You will therefore need to consult the PROB 6 finding-aid to find the piece number for 1822, not 1825, and, since the place of residence is given as *Pts*, that is, relating to someone who died abroad or at sea, you will turn to the Registrar's seat which dealt with such cases and then to the month of October (see chapter 1.3 and appendix A).

1.5 PROB 9: Special and limited probates

These two examples are taken from the PROB 12 volume for 1825:

For most years of the nineteenth century (1800, 1802-1804, 1806-1858) if the entry in the PROB 12 Calendar says 'Limited Probate' or 'Special Probate' you will find an extended probate act in PROB 9 which will supplement the information in the will. PROB 9 is not on microfilm and so it can only be read at Kew, but you will enjoy being able to handle a real book. You order it on the document ordering computer.

Each book in PROB 9 is divided into sections by seats in the same way as the administration act books in PROB 6, described above. It is also written in ordinary handwriting, and the grants are 'entered at length' (E.A.L.). You may find as many as twenty pages relating to one grant - but they may be very tedious and repetitive, relating perhaps to property indentures.

1.6 PROB 7: Special and limited administrations

From 1810, PROB 7 contains the special and limited administrations 'entered at length'. It is arranged in 'seats' and months, like PROB 6, but has not been filmed and so, like PROB 9, it is ordered on the computer and you can read the original book but only at Kew.

However, until 1810, all administrations are in PROB 6. If you find the abbreviation 'E.A.L.' in the ordinary roughly alphabetical sequence this means that the record of the grant of administration has been 'entered at length' and will usually be found at the beginning of the section for that month. If you do not find it there, search around, at first within the section for that seat, but if necessary, in other parts of the same piece. Entries sometimes became displaced.

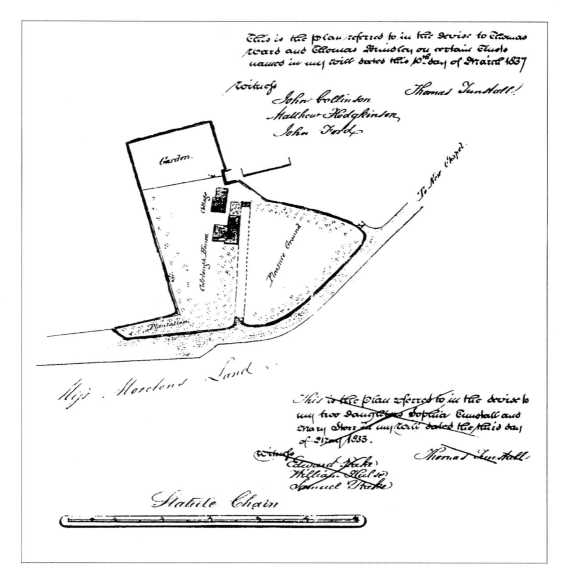

Fig.8   An example of a plan defining a property recorded in a will register. PROB 11/1928, f 212 RH.

Admons 1837

Small	Robert	Pts	July
Merch Ship Orient			
Sawdon	Robert	Pts	Aug
Merch Ship Charlotte			
Spain	George	Pts	Aug
Belvidera			
Scott	John	Pts	Aug
Serjt Major 6t Regt of Foot			
Silvett	Joseph	Pts	Octr
East India Comps Ship Asia			
Silverthorne	James	Pts	Octr
Serjt Major 56t Regt of Foot			
Santiero	Edward	Pts	Novr
Swartz	John	Pts	Novr
Merch Ship Robarts			
Sayer	Thomas	Pts	Novr
Cruizer			
Simmonds Richard John		Surrey & Pts	Decr
Merch Ship Lowther			
Soper	Robert	Notts	Decr
10t Hussars			

Wills

Taylor	Thomas	Pts	Mch
Marine Gannet			

Fig. 9 A page from the list of non-commissioned soldiers and sailors in the PROB 12 volume for 1837.

19

2 The Eighteenth Century

2.1 Indexes

Eighteenth-century wills and administrations are now almost completely indexed by personal name of the deceased.

2.1.1 Wills 1750-1800

These are covered by Anthony Camp's index (see bibliography) and he is working on the administrations. Progress can be followed by reading 'Diary of a Genealogist' in *Family Tree* magazine.

The wills index for the first time achieved the monumental task of combining a fifty-year period in one union index. You can conveniently look up all the entries for one surname for the whole period and then find the PROB 11 piece numbers in the class list. The index is in six volumes. The last volume has an appendix containing corrections of numerous errors in the first two volumes (containing letters A-C) which have been discovered since publication.

2.1.2 Wills and administrations 1701-1749

These wills and administrations are being indexed by the Friends of the Public Record Office (FPRO), and by the time you read this, volumes for all these years will be on the shelves. When the work is finished a complete union index, in one single alphabetical series, will be published. This index has the great advantage that it gives you the piece numbers for both PROB 11 and PROB 6 so that you can go straight to the film without having to consult the class lists. These films can be read in the central London reading room as well as at Kew.

In this index 'sig' (the abbreviation of 'signature') indicates the quire number, eg:
    ARNOLD Richard 1740 Feb London PROB 11/700, sig 29

To read this will, help yourself to the film containing PROB 11/700 and turn to quire number 29.

The index has been compiled by volunteers working on individual years. Much checking has been done, but if you find any errors or omissions the editors would be glad to know, so please tell the officer on duty in the reading room.

2.1.3 Administrations 1750-1800

For the time being you will need to use the PROB 12 calendars as an index to administrations in the years 1750-1800. See chapter 1, sections 1, 3 and 4. Alternatively, the Society of Genealogists will search their index for a fee. Their address is given in Appendix B, section C3.

2.2 The arrangement of the act books in the eighteenth century

Although the PCC's business had been organized according to the seat system since 1719, the arrangement of the act books described in chapter 1 and appendix A did not begin until 1744, so the situation in the eighteenth century is as follows:

> Until **1719**, although a division into seats is discernible, you will need to search the whole month, as there is no knowing in which section the grant you are looking for may appear.

> Between **1719** and **1743** the act books are arranged by month and then by seat, so that the entries for January for every seat will be given before any entries for February.

> From **1744** the act books are arranged by seat and then by month, with all the entries for the Registrar's seat preceding those for the Surrey seat, and so on, just as they do in the nineteenth century.

> From **1719** the name of the clerk of the seat usually appears at the head of each section.

In the eighteenth century all the administrations (including the limited grants) are in PROB 6 which is on microfilm and so can be read in the central London reading room as well as at Kew.

2.3 Latin probate clauses and grants of administration

Fortunately in the eighteenth century wills were almost always written in English, but until 1733 you will find the probate clauses and grants of administration in Latin. If you are working backwards in your research you will by then be familiar with the usual wording of these grants and will soon be able to pick out the words you need, probably just the names, places and relationships. There are several simple guides to Latin for family historians, and some are suggested in the bibliography.

An example of an administration from 1720 is given below with a transcription in which the abbreviations have been expanded. This is followed by a translation. You can see that if you pick out the words starting with capital letters in the Latin text, you will have the information you need. You already know the year and month of the grant (from the index in which you found the reference) and so the exact day of the month, which is the only indication of date within the grant, will probably not be important to you.

Latin acts of probate and administration

Here is an example of an administration from 1720 (PROB 6/96, f 98 LH):

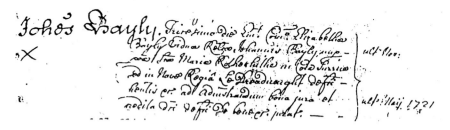

The dates in the right hand margin indicate that the **inventory** (see glossary and chapter 9) was to be exhibited by the last day of November and the **account** (see glossary) to be returned by the final day of May 1721.

Johannes Bayly. Tricesimo die Emanavit Commissio Elizabethae Bayly viduae Relictae Johannis Bayly nuper parochiae Sanctae Mariae Rotherhithe in Comitatu Surriae sed in Nave Regia Le Dreadnought defuncti habentis &c [dum vixit et mortis suae tempore bona jura sive credita in diversis diocesibus sive peculiaribus jurisdictionibus sufficientia ad fundandum jurisdictionem Curiae Praerogativae Cantuariensis] ad Administrandum bona jura et credita dicti defuncti De bene &c. [et fideliter administrando eadem ad sancta Dei evangelia] juratae
    ultimus [dies] Novembris
    ultimus [dies] Maij 1721

John Bayly. On the thirtieth day a commission was issued to Elizabeth Bayly widow relict of John Bayly formerly of the parish of Saint Mary Rotherhithe in the county of Surrey but in the royal ship The Dreadnought deceased having etc. [while he lived and at the time of his death goods rights or credits in different dioceses or peculiar jurisdictions sufficient to found the jurisdiction of the Prerogative Court of Canterbury] to administer the goods rights and credits of the said deceased having been sworn [on the holy gospels] to well etc. and [faithfully administer the same]
    final [day] of November
    final [day] of May 1721

Although the probate clauses are in Latin until 1733, you will find many wills are written in extremely down-to-earth English, expressing very deeply-felt wishes.

For example, Dorothy Ann Thornycroft felt the need to add this postscript to her will which she dated 'May the 12 17016'(!) and which was proved 10 July 1719 (PROB 11/569, sig 138):

> Bury me as privately and cheap as you can and where you will for it is pretty equal to me where only desire as little as can to be spent on it

Here is the complete will of Elizabeth Dungey dated 4 February 1761:

Will of Elizabeth Dungey   PROB 11/864, sig 126

> This is to certifie all it may concern that the India stock in my name is my neice Elizabeth Digords and that I give her all my wearing cloth and Linnen whatever besides this appears to be mine I give to be equally divided between her and her sister Ann Hinckley. I desire to be buried in the Churchyard wherever I Dye if in Town with a Hearse and one coach if in the country to be carried by the parish Barire to the ground without Pall Bearers I owe no Body Sixpence in the World

Witnesses: Eliz. Burniston, Catherine Nicholls.

Here is an example of a nuncupative, or oral, will, made in circumstances where writing was clearly impossible!

> Memorandum that James Dixon late Mariner... in his Majesties Sloop Jane, Batchelor, deceased, did on or about the 22nd of November 1718 in the Morning of the said day being in the hold of the sd [vessel] and then about to engage with a pirate called the Adventure Sloop did in the presence of severall credible witnesses utter and declare his last Will and Testament Nuncupative or by word of mouth in the words following viz: Messmate (being going to engage) who knows whether of us shall live but if it please God it is my misfortune to dye first I desire that you would take care and demand all my Wages Prize Money and what shall be due to me from this day and the longest liver of us to take all. And the same ship being half an hour after engaged by the enemy the said James Dixon received a Shott who immediately dyed.

This will was proved in December 1719 (PROB 11/571, sig 231).

Limited administrations sometimes contain interesting details of the business affairs of the deceased. This entry from PROB 6/107 (folios 2RH - 6LH) caught the eye of one of the volunteers when she was checking for the FPRO index:

By what Ships received	Marks	Quantity	By whom shipped
	W L	1	Doctor William Levingstone
	I C	1	Joseph Godwin
	HS	2	Josiah Simonds
	I R	2	Roger Ingram
	I M	2	John Morris
	I M	2	
	R	2	John Daughtry
	R W	1	Robert Wethe
	D Bank	2	John Dean
	P I	1	John Porter
	I	1	John Side
	N K	2	Nicholas Kington
	S B	2	Symkin Bryant
	IS	2	Jethro Sumner
	E	1	John Eaton
The Sally Cap John Morren from Virginia		78 hhds	
	N C	1	Solomon Wilson
	E P	1	Dr Robert Phillipson
	T T	1	Chichley Corbin Thacker

This table forms part of the limited administration of John Midford, January 1731. It is a copy of a tobacco import schedule drawn up for the Commissioners of Customs and dated November 1730. The symbols are the cask marks of individual tobacco growers in Virginia, Maryland and Antigua, who had sent their hogsheads of tobacco to John Midford for sale in the port of London. Listed is each planter (mostly from Virginia) and each ship transporting the goods, often with the captain's name. Eleven vessels, including one frigate, carried 492 hogsheads of tobacco.

This very unusual administration was limited to this unsold tobacco as it was in danger of perishing. Two other grants on the rest of his goods were made at later dates. For further details see Elizabeth Hull's article in *Prophile*, Vol 3 No 2, Autumn 1992, pages 28-29.

The examples given on page 23 from the wills of Dorothy Thornycroft and Elizabeth Dungey should be sufficient to show you that wills of ordinary people can be found in the PCC even before the nineteenth century. And a rough check of some of the entries for wills and administrations in the first half of the eighteenth century shows that nearly twenty per cent related to the estates of women.

3. Before 1700

3.1 Indexes

There are printed indexes for all PCC wills up to 1700 and details are given in appendix B.

There are indexes for administrations up to 1664, but 1661 is incomplete. An index for 1665 to 1700 is in preparation. Meanwhile use PROB 12 (see chapter 1, section 1).

Copies of the printed indexes can be found in many libraries. The PROB 11 and PROB 6 class lists will enable you to convert the references in the indexes into PRO piece numbers so that you can select the film you need. In some of the printed indexes the reference will be to the name of the register rather than to the year (see page 14). In this case you can use either the list in appendix C of this book or the one in the PROB 11 class list to convert this name into a date.

3.2 The Civil War and the Commonwealth Period

The Civil War severely disrupted the organization of probate business. For a short period a second court acting as the PCC was held in Oxford, but the records were subsequently united with those of the London court, so you should look for wills during this period in the usual way.

During the Commonwealth period there were no ecclesiastical courts functioning in England and Wales. Between 1653 and the Restoration in 1660 all probate jurisdiction was administered by a single court of civil commission in London and its records are to be found with those of the PCC.

For some wills proved in the period 1643 to 1646 there are no surviving register copies in PROB 11 and therefore you will need to read the original wills which are in class PROB 10: see chapter 5. The appendix to the introductory note to the PROB 10 class list will help you to find them.

From 1651 to 1660 the act books and the probate clauses were written in English.

4. PROB 8: Probate Act Books

Class PROB 8 contains the probate act books. It is not much used by family historians but perhaps it should be. It sometimes gives a later place of residence than that given in the will, and perhaps more than one, for example:

> OSBALDESTON, Edith 1842 Nov 765   PROB 12 gives Dorset as her place of residence but the will says she is of Brighton, Sussex. The entry in PROB 8 explains that Edith Osbaldeston was 'formerly of Brighton, Sussex, then of Cheshunt Herts, but late of Weymouth, Spinster.'

PROB 8 may also give the details of a subsequent grant of probate on the will if the details do not appear as a marginal note at the end of the will in PROB 11. These subsequent grants are often placed at the <u>end</u> of the entries for each month, in a second alphabetical series.

Occasionally you may find an occupation or description (such as 'Widow') of the testator given in PROB 8 which is not given in the will.

From 1796 a rough valuation of the estate (often subsequently amended) appears in the margin. This was the result of the imposition of the taxes commonly known as death duties (see chapter 8).

Limited and special probates for 1781, 1800, 1802-1804 and from 1806-1858 are in PROB 9.

The example on page 27, illustrating the letters I and J, is taken from PROB 8.

PROB 8 is not on film and can only be read at Kew.

The Letters I and J

The letters I and J are treated as one letter in the PCC records and you will find names beginning with these letters mixed up together. If you are looking for a name beginning with I, do not stop when you come to one beginning with J. In the example below, taken from PROB 8/248, Surrey Seat, you will see that Jackson is followed by Isbell and James is followed by Ilsley.

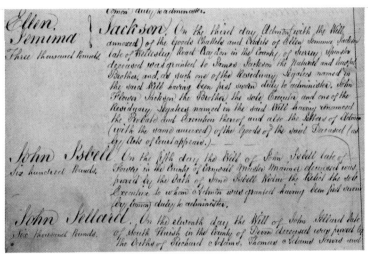

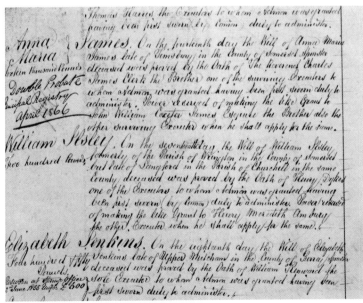

Fig 10   An example of the treatment of the letters I and J in the records of the PCC. PROB 8/248 Surrey Seat.

27

5. PROB 10: Original Wills

Class PROB 10 holds the original wills. You are unlikely to need to look at them unless you particularly want to see the signature of the testator, or one of the witnesses, or you have reason to suspect that the clerk who made the register copy (which is in PROB 11) made a mistake.

It is also possible that where the meaning of a passage in the PROB 11 copy of the will is not clear, the original will may clarify it. In some instances there is punctuation in the original which was not copied by the PCC clerk.

PROB 10 is not on film and will continue to be kept on another site after January 1997, and so several days' notice is required before the wills can be produced (at Kew only). You will need to know the month of probate when ordering. This is done on the computer.

When the will is in the testator's own handwriting, it may reveal a personality which is not evident in the uniformity of PROB 11. See, for example, the will of Betty Smith reproduced as pages 30-31.

You may like to compare the original with the extract from PROB 11 (PROB 11/ 1922, f 66 RH) and the transcription given opposite.

In most cases, however, the original will would have been written by a professional scribe. And note that not all original wills survive, while some so-called 'originals' are themselves copies.

The will of Betty Smith proved 18 January 1840, PROB 10/5903

> this is my last request wich ihave to make ibequeath to John smith my son the sum of one hundred pound now in the hands of my Brother James Judd in the town of rugby and allso all my goods and chattles ihave about me (all except silver spoons too my Brother James) or to his successors iallso wish willam smith my grandson to have my clock and John smith my watch and my cloaths and linnen to bee devided betwen marry smith and willams wife only if mrs underwood is alive let her have my Black Bonnet one shall and chect apron and what old things you dont like to ware give away to anybody you like let nothing be sold and ialls request imay bee buried in flanell and let everything bee done with as little expence as possible for iwish to have everything very plain only put me into the grave where my late husband is put and dont let the gravestone bee alterd for iwish to have no expence as can bee avidid
>
> and when all expences of my fewnarall and everything is paid what their is remaning of my late legacy let it bee devided between william smith my grandson and my Brother James Judd of the town of Rugby and ihope all things will bee settled agreeable to you all wittness this my Hand Betty smith of the town of northamton sined by my own hand 11 of janary 1839 Betty smith.

This is an example of an *administration (with the will annexed)* (see chapter 1.2.3). No executor or residuary legatee was named in the will, so *administration (with the will annexed)* was granted to 'William Smith the lawful Grandson and next of kin of the Deceased'.

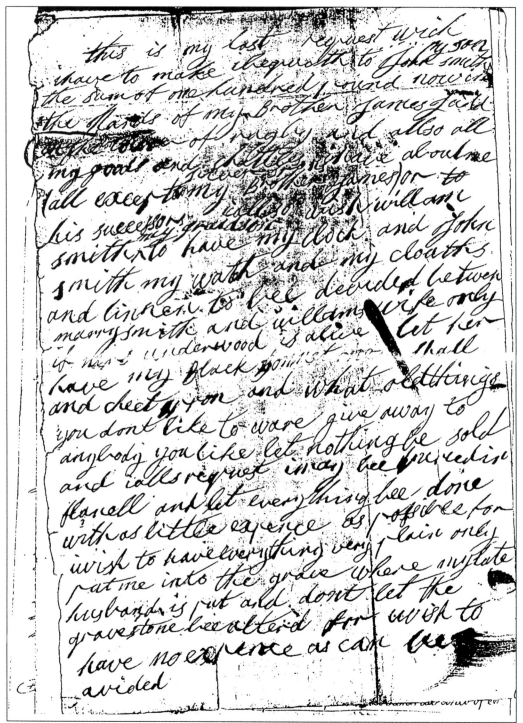

Fig 11   An example of an original will in the testator's own handwriting. PROB 10/5903.

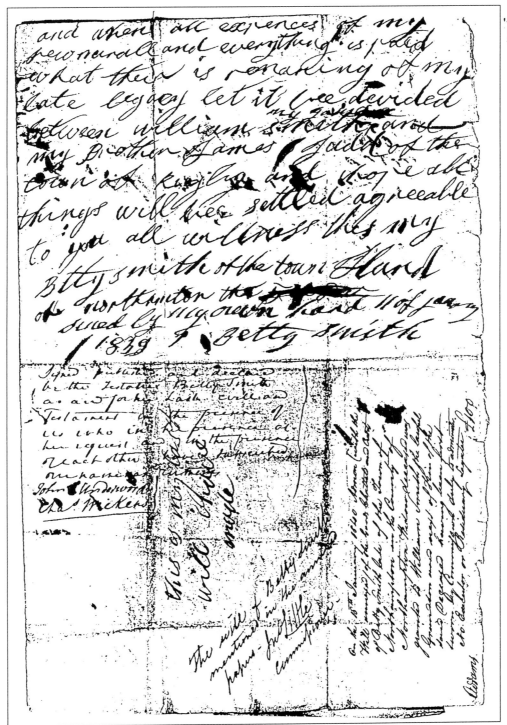

Fig 11   An example of an original will in the testator's own handwriting. PROB 10/5903.

6. Litigation in the PCC

Although this guide does not set out to explain the complexities of litigation in the PCC, descriptions of two cases involving disputed wills will briefly illustrate the type of material which might be found and the procedure by which you might find it.

> Note that all the documents mentioned in this chapter, except those in PROB 6 and PROB 11, are read as original documents and only at Kew.

6.1 By Interlocutory Decree

You may have noticed 'By Int. Dec.' or a similar abbreviation in the left hand margin beside a few of the entries in PROB 12, and have wondered how you would follow this up. It must be emphasized that it often seems to be a matter of chance whether any relevant records survived, and in many cases you will find nothing. But the first places to look are among the pleadings in disputed cases in PROB 18 and among the main series of exhibits in PROB 31. The procedure is best illustrated by a case study. There is a card index to the documents in PROB 18 of the personal names of persons whose wills were subject to litigation and the class is therefore easy to search. Looking for references to PROB 31 may be more time-consuming, though the card index to inventories in this class can sometimes provide a short-cut. See appendix D.

The case of William Slyfield

Document references:

PROB 12 for 1831 Aug	Administration By Int.Decree
PROB 6/207 (1831) Aug	Administration Registrar's Seat f 39 LH
PROB 6/214 (1838) Nov	Administration Surrey Seat f 136 LH
PROB 18/124, number 35	Pleadings in case of *Slyfield v.Slyfield*
PROB 31/1281/1400-1403	Exhibits in case of *Slyfield v.Slyfield*
PROB 30/302	Acts of court book
PROB 11/1883, sig 628 (August 1837)	Will of Elizabeth Slyfield, Widow

The entry in PROB 12 has the marginal note: By Int. (ie Interlocutory) Decree. This means that the will was disputed in the PCC and there is therefore a chance that something relating to the case may have survived in the litigation records of the PCC, so it is worth looking to see. But first let us look at the usual entry in PROB 6/207, f 39 LH.

You will see that there is a later marginal addition referring to a grant of administration of goods left unadministered in November 1838. This is probably the result of the death of the administrator (usually a relative or a creditor) and indeed we find (in PROB 6/214, the administration act book for 1838) 'goods left unadministered by Elizabeth Slyfield Widow deceased'. So it is now worth looking for her will, and sure enough the will of Elizabeth Slyfield was proved in July 1837.

Note that in this particular case there is no hint in PROB 6 of the interlocutory decree. It is only PROB 12 which gives you this information. But because the administration was the subject of litigation it was granted in the Registrar's seat, not in the Surrey seat which was usual for Dorset. The marginal note helpfully informs you that the subsequent grant is to be found in the Surrey seat.

PROB 18 contains *Allegations*. There is a card index in two parts, the first of names of plaintiffs, the second of causes. In the first, under Slyfield, is the entry:

SLYFIELD William Weymouth Dorset
    SLYFIELD con SLYFIELD et al 1830 124/35

To read this document (at Kew), order PROB 18/124 on the computer. When you receive the bundle, which looks like a brown paper parcel, and consists of folded foolscap documents, look for number 35. This consists of an allegation, a document produced as a result of a legal dispute between the widow of the deceased and his children. The allegation was rejected. Since it refers to exhibits in PROB 31 the allegation and exhibits need to be studied together, so you may wish to order photocopies to peruse at your leisure at home.

PROB 31 contains exhibits brought into court in contested causes. It includes a variety of documents such as proxies, affidavits, commissions, elections of guardians for minors, inventories, wills, codicils and other testamentary papers.

On the shelf in the reading-room you will find a book index entitled *PROB 31 Index to Wills*. It is in two parts. The first part is a modern alphabetical list of names with references to <u>page</u> numbers in the second list where the references for ordering the documents will be found.

In the first part, the alphabetical list, under Slyfield we find the reference 188. So then we turn to page 188 of the second list which gives:

> 1281/1403 Slyfield, William, Melcombe Regis, within borough and town of Weymouth & Melcombe Regis, co. Dorset. (1) Will, 1829, in book (2) Like (3) Com[mission] 7 Jul 1830 (4) Affid[avit] 9 Jul 1830, 2ff (13 July 1830).

Numbers (1) and (2) are the books marked A and B referred to in the allegation in PROB 18.

This document can then be ordered on the computer. After entering PROB 31 and the first part of the piece number 1281 press / and enter the sub number 1403.

It is also worth seeing whether there are any other exhibits relating to the case. The index to PROB 31 is in PROB 33 of which there are copies in a set of black books in chronological order which you will find on the shelf. Since you know that the case was heard in July 1830, take down the volume for 1830-1832. At the front you will find a list of surnames which is the index for 1830. (It is followed later in the book by indexes for 1831 and 1832. You have to deduce this as they are untitled.) The names are indexed under initial letter only, so it is necessary to look at all the surnames beginning with S. Wm Slyfield is the second name on the fifth page of the names beginning with S. Here are references to three more documents, numbers 1400-1402. If you had not already got the piece number for July 1830 from the list of wills in PROB 31 you would need to look it up in the class list for PROB 31. Make a note of the month, July, as every month has its own number. You can now order these documents too, in the way described above.

If there had been no will listed in the PROB 31 index of wills you would have had no way of knowing the exact date to look for. You would then have had to start at the date of the decree (in this case 1831) in PROB 33 and work backwards.

The allegation shows that the widow hoped to have the book marked B (PROB 31/ 1281/1403, 2) proved as the will. In the two proxies, PROB 31/1281/1400 and

PROB 31/1281/1401, the widow appoints F H Dyke, notary public, to *propound* the validity of the said will, and the children appoint P C Toker, notary public, to *oppose* the validity of the said will. These proxies contain witnessed signatures of the widow and of the three children and the son-in-law.

Book A is a small notebook in which William Slyfield kept, somewhat haphazardly, records of his financial dealings and wishes concerning his will. His descendants would no doubt be thrilled to handle an article of such personal significance and in his own handwriting. For example: 'I have bought a house at Kingsclere and Mr Reeves [his son-in -law] is to pay me Nine Pounds per year and all Tax's except Land Tax.'

The allegation states that on his deathbed he asked for book A to be thrown onto the fire. However, this was not done. He then dictated his wishes to his eldest son, and these are written in the book marked B. He attempted to sign his name there but his hand was so tremulous that he was unable to do so. Nevertheless he himself locked up the book marked B in his iron chest for safety.

For most readers, the interest of this document lies in the glimpses of family life which it provides, describing the comings and goings in William Slyfield's sickroom, and how, three days before he died, and being very ill, and his eldest son Joseph having arrived, he exclaimed 'Thank God Joseph is come, I will settle my affairs'. This he signally failed to do!

Unfortunately only the widow's side of the case seems to have survived. PROB 30 *Acts of court* gives the final decisions of the court but PROB 30/302, for July 1830, adds little to the information provided in the other documents. It refers to 'William Slyfield deceased without having made any Will or testamentary paper valid in Law'. The case was heard on Thursday 22 July 1830 in the Common Hall of Doctors' Commons London, 'on which day F H Dyke prayed his Allegation to be admitted. Toker prayed the same to be rejected. The Judge having read the Allegation and heard Advocates and Proctors on both sides rejected the Allegation' and granted letters of administration to Elizabeth Slyfield, widow, the relict of the said deceased.

No document has been found which supports the rejection of the allegation, there being no surviving document in this case in PROB 25, which contains the *answers* made by defendants to the allegations.

There is no sign in Elizabeth Slyfield's will made six years later that the dispute had left any acrimony. She makes numerous detailed bequests to her children and grandchildren, right down to 'the likeness of his father on horseback' to a grandson, and allotting the eggcups and toastrack, and she makes her eldest son an executor.

It must be emphasized that when you start out to follow up a *By Int.Dec.* entry, you should be prepared for disappointment. Of twenty such entries in *Dorset Wills and Administrations in the PCC 1821-1858*, there were entries in the PROB 18 card index for only three, and in the PROB 31 wills index only for William Slyfield. There were entries for eight of the twenty in the index to PROB 37 and for five in that for PROB 26. There remain seven of these cases for which there are no entries in any of these indexes. But if you are lucky, you may be very lucky indeed.

> Note: Some readers may prefer to search PROB 37 and PROB 26 before using PROB 33 as those classes have alphabetical indexes by deceased, which are bound with the class lists.

6.2 By Sentence

Sentences record the verdicts of the judges of the PCC in cases of disputed grants of probate and administration. The two opposing parties to a cause would submit their own versions of sentences to the judge of the court, who would promulgate, that is confirm, the sentence that accorded with his verdict, and the victorious party would pay for the sentence to be registered in the will registers (PROB 11).

The case of Elizabeth Chapman

In PROB 12 under Wills 1835:

By Sentence   CHAPMAN   Elizabeth   Dorset   Jan   9
Probate Clause at end of will: PROB 11/1841, sig 9

> Proved at London with a codicil 13 Jany 1835 before the Judge by the Oath of Hephzibah Flight Widow the surviving executor to whom Admon was granted being first sworn by comm[ission] duly to administer a Definitive sentence in writing having been first read signed promulged and given for the force and validity of the said will and codicil as by Acts of Court appears.

PROB 8/228 January 1835 Registrar's Seat
Elizabeth Chapman £30,000 By Sentence

> On the 13th day the will with a Codicil of Elizabeth Chapman formerly of Lyme Regis but late of Chideock Spinster deceased was proved by the Oath of... (the rest identical with the probate clause at end of will, above).

At this stage it is better to ignore the mention of acts of court and go straight to the depositions in PROB 26 and the indexes to exhibits in PROB 33, there being no entry for Elizabeth Chapman in either the PROB 18 card index to allegations or the PROB 31 list of wills.

PROB 26 *Depositions* bound by suit 1826-1857, indexed by deceased and by plaintiff. The index gives:

PROB 26/138 Chapman Elizabeth (*Flight con Gibbs et al*)
Flight con Gibbs et al is the name of the case. You already know from the probate clause that Hephzibah Flight, Widow, is the surviving executor. You will soon discover from the documents that David Gibbs is one of the 'cousins german' who disputed the will on the grounds of the alleged insanity of the testator. PROB 26/ 138 is read as an original document at Kew and is ordered on the computer.

On the cover of PROB 26/138 you will find:

> The depositions (bound into a book) in the case of
> *Flight v Gibbs and others*
> Depositions on the Allegations given by both proctors.
> Index inside.

The index is a loose paper giving a list of witnesses, with their occupations and ages. There are two lists: one of the witnesses on the allegation given by Addams (who represented Flight) dated 5 May 1834, and the other of those on the allegation by Wheeler (who represented Gibbs) dated 14 June 1834.

Part of the case for Flight was that the witnesses to the will, who included a surgeon, would not have witnessed the will and codicil had they had any doubt as to the sanity of the deceased.

The case for Gibbs was that the deceased's lunacy was well known and well documented. One of his witnesses kept an asylum and had cared for the deceased.

PROB 33 *Index to Exhibits* 1833-1835
1834. Under Chapman Elizabeth the index gives a long list of documents in this case, most of which are marked with an asterisk to indicate that they are now in PROB 37.

PROB 37 *Cause Papers* Later Series. The typescript index with the class list gives:

PROB 37	Date	
		Chapman Elizabeth
		formerly of Lyme Regis, Dorset late of
		Chideock, Dorset, spinster.
898	1834	*Flight v Gibbs and others*

(898 is the piece number in PROB 37).

A footnote says:

> This bundle contains three notebooks containing journals for 1801-1815, particularly detailing the life of Tiverton Baptist Church, Wellington Baptist Church and Lyme Regis Baptist Church.

PROB 37/898

The whole bundle concerns this case. These are the exhibits that were brought into court as evidence in support of the depositions. Even a brief examination shows that there is a tremendous amount of genealogical information to be gathered here. All the deceased's cousins german, her only next-of-kin, are listed, including David Gibbs. Her age, father, dates of birth and death, are also mentioned. There are certificates and correspondence concerning her lunacy.

Books B and C of the notebooks mentioned above are her own personal diaries, but book A is an account of events and meetings at these three Baptist Churches and includes lists of members as follows:

> Tiverton, Devon 1800-1805
> Wellington, Somerset 1807-1810
> Lyme Regis, Dorset 1810-1812

No doubt there is a wealth of other material equally valuable to family and local history waiting to be discovered in this class.

For the sake of completeness you may wish to look at PROB 30 which contains the acts of court and is arranged in monthly bundles. The class list gives the piece numbers and the relevant document is found in PROB 30/323 (1834 Nov-Dec). However, it is not a very interesting or informative document, merely confirming that the case was decided in favour of Hephzibah Flight.

PROB 30/323 *Acts of court* 18 December 1834
Flight v. Gibbs and Others

A business of granting a Probate of the last will and testament with a codicil of Elizabeth Chapman to Hephzibah Flight Widow the surviving Executor named in the will.

In pain of parties cited thrice called and not appearing Addams porrected a definitive sentence... The Judge having read the evidence and heard Advocates and Proctors on both sides therein read signed promulged and gave the sentence by him the said Addams... for the force and validity of the said will ... and decreed a Probate thereof to the said Hephzibah Flight Widow.

Wadeson for Wheeler praying Justice and at the further petition of Wadeson for Wheeler and Addams directed the Expences on both sides to be paid out of the Estate of the said deceased.

7. A Note on Nonconformists with an example of a family tree based on PCC wills

There is a recently published PRO Readers' Guide to nonconformist records (see bibliography). This chapter is only designed to show how wills can supplement other research in this difficult area.

In many families there have been periods of some degree of nonconformity. In a case where records of birth or baptism, marriage and burial are sparse a good series of wills can supply the structure of a family tree even if some of the dates are missing. The example opposite shows how this was done for the Weedon family where PCC probate records were found for five generations. The references to Quakers and Baptists are an indication of why so few parish register entries have been found, but this is more than compensated for by the detail contained in the wills. As a result, a family history can be compiled far richer than a mere genealogy.

Until they were introduced to the PCC wills, this family had only the portrait of Timothy Weedon (1771-1851) reproduced on page 42, some silver, and the rather patchy results of their searches in Berkshire parish registers and Newbury records. From this series of wills they have been able to build a rich picture of the personalities and possessions of their ancestors.

It was Ann Weedon's will, proved in the PCC in 1779, asking that she be buried in the Quaker burial ground in Newbury 'if they will permit it', that led to the discovery of the record of her burial, one of very few births or baptisms, marriages or burials discovered when this research was carried out in 1987-1989.

It was John Cox, Ann Weedon's father, who left her the property in Bartholomew Street, Newbury. The family continued to live in this street for another two generations.

Ann leaves to each of her children two silver table spoons, and to her daughter Ann Gleed 'my Silver Salver and Buff-coloured Damask Gown', while her daughter Joan was to have 'my black Paduasoy suit of cloaths'. Paduasoy was a strong corded silk fabric.

John Weedon, whose will was proved in 1804, went into great detail about the disposition of his belongings. He lists several books (mostly religious) and a great deal of silver marked J W, as well as a white cornelian ring which he leaves to his daughter Rachel, and to his eldest son a mourning ring 'which was his grandfather Cox's'. His shoe buckles, sleeve buckles, buttons and studs are all allocated.

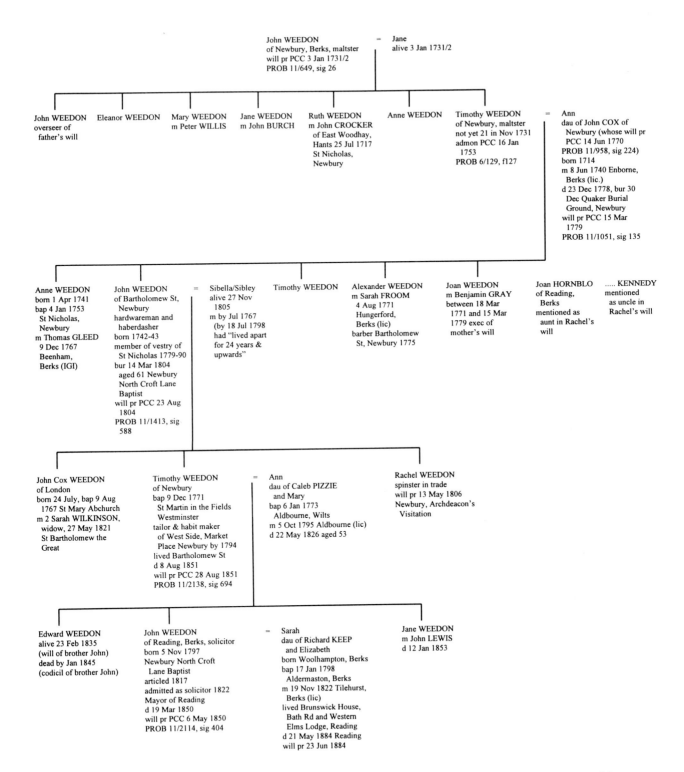

John WEEDON
of Newbury, Berks, maltster
will pr PCC 3 Jan 1731/2
PROB 11/649, sig 26
= Jane
alive 3 Jan 1731/2

John WEEDON
overseer of
father's will

Eleanor WEEDON

Mary WEEDON
m Peter WILLIS

Jane WEEDON
m John BURCH

Ruth WEEDON
m John CROCKER
of East Woodhay,
Hants 25 Jul 1717
St Nicholas,
Newbury

Anne WEEDON

Timothy WEEDON
of Newbury, maltster
not yet 21 in Nov 1731
admon PCC 16 Jan
1753
PROB 6/129, f127
= Ann
dau of John COX of
Newbury (whose will pr
PCC 14 Jun 1770
PROB 11/958, sig 224)
born 1714
m 8 Jun 1740 Enborne,
Berks (lic.)
d 23 Dec 1778, bur 30
Dec Quaker Burial
Ground, Newbury
will pr PCC 15 Mar
1779
PROB 11/1051, sig 135

Anne WEEDON
born 1 Apr 1741
bap 4 Jan 1753
St Nicholas,
Newbury
m Thomas GLEED
9 Dec 1767
Beenham,
Berks (IGI)

John WEEDON
of Bartholomew St,
Newbury
hardwareman and
haberdasher
born 1742-43
member of vestry of
St Nicholas 1779-90
bur 14 Mar 1804
aged 61 Newbury
North Croft Lane
Baptist
will pr PCC 23 Aug
1804
PROB 11/1413, sig
588
= Sibella/Sibley
alive 27 Nov
1805
m by Jul 1767
(by 18 Jul 1798
had "lived apart
for 24 years &
upwards"

Timothy WEEDON

Alexander WEEDON
m Sarah FROOM
4 Aug 1771
Hungerford,
Berks (lic)
barber Bartholomew
St, Newbury 1775

Joan WEEDON
m Benjamin GRAY
between 18 Mar
1771 and 15 Mar
1779 exec of
mother's will

Joan HORNBLO
of Reading,
Berks
mentioned as
aunt in Rachel's
will

..... KENNEDY
mentioned
as uncle in
Rachel's will

John Cox WEEDON
of London
born 24 July, bap 9 Aug
1767 St Mary Abchurch
m 2 Sarah WILKINSON,
widow, 27 May 1821
St Bartholomew the
Great

Timothy WEEDON
of Newbury
bap 9 Dec 1771
St Martin in the Fields
Westminster
tailor & habit maker
of West Side, Market
Place Newbury by 1794
lived Bartholomew St
d 8 Aug 1851
will pr PCC 28 Aug 1851
PROB 11/2138, sig 694
= Ann
dau of Caleb PIZZIE
and Mary
bap 6 Jan 1773
Aldbourne, Wilts
m 5 Oct 1795 Aldbourne (lic)
d 22 May 1826 aged 53

Rachel WEEDON
spinster in trade
will pr 13 May 1806
Newbury, Archdeacon's
Visitation

Edward WEEDON
alive 23 Feb 1835
(will of brother John)
dead by Jan 1845
(codicil of brother John)

John WEEDON
of Reading, Berks, solicitor
born 5 Nov 1797
Newbury North Croft
Lane Baptist
articled 1817
admitted as solicitor 1822
Mayor of Reading
d 19 Mar 1850
will pr PCC 6 May 1850
PROB 11/2114, sig 404
= Sarah
dau of Richard KEEP
and Elizabeth
born Woolhampton, Berks
bap 17 Jan 1798
Aldermaston, Berks
m 19 Nov 1822 Tilehurst,
Berks (lic)
lived Brunswick House,
Bath Rd and Western
Elms Lodge, Reading
d 21 May 1884 Reading
will pr 23 Jun 1884

Jane WEEDON
m John LEWIS
d 12 Jan 1853

41

'I also direct my said son John Cox Weedon to pay unto my executors all such monies as I have paid or shall pay for or towards the maintenance of his illegitimate child at Colnbrook'. 'If my wife Sibilly from whom for her Incontinence [ie infidelity] I have lived apart for twenty four years and upward should make any Claim upon my Effects I give to her one shilling only.'

In his daughter Rachel's will (this one was proved in Newbury at the Archdeacon's Visitation in 1806 and is now in Berkshire county record office) the white cornelian ring is left to her brother Timothy and she divides the silver marked J W which she had inherited from her father between her nephew John and her niece Jane. His son Timothy, whose will was proved in 1851, left to his servant Sarah May 'ten pounds and my rose pattern china tea service of white and gold' before disposing of the rest of his property among his family.

Fig 12   Portrait of Timothy Weedon.

Unfortunately the will of Timothy's son, John Weedon, proved in 1850 contained no personal details in four pages of wordy legal jargon, and in this case one had to turn to the death duty entry (see chapter 8) to discover the names of all his children. His widow, too, left an impersonal will, no doubt drawn up in her husband's office, but added her own personal note giving instructions to her son for the welfare of her carriage horse known by the name of Jim and her dog Rover.

Until a recent burglary John's descendants still had the silver marked J W, and it had been planned to include a photograph of it here. Fortunately the thieves did not take the portrait of Timothy.

Here is an extract from the original will of John Weedon proved in August 1804, (PROB 10/3677).

I give my Books as follow, namely, to my said Son John Cox Weedon, the Prodigal Son, the Book of Martyrs, and a Bible in 4to to my said Daughter Rachel Josephus, a Bible, and Pool's Annotations in two Volumes Folio; to my said Son Timothy Howard's Cyclopædia in three Volumes Folio, and a Concordance.

8. The Death Duty Registers as a finding aid to wills and administrations

As mentioned in the introduction, if any of the taxes known collectively as death duties were paid, the death duty register records the name of the court where the will was proved or the administration granted. From 1796 legacy duty was payable on legacies and the residues of personal estate worth more than £20 but until 1805 close relatives (spouses, children, parents and grandparents) were exempt, so relatively few estates paid duty between these dates. However, the scope of the duty was gradually extended so that by 1815, when inherited property worth over £100 became liable, most estates were subject to tax, and until 1858 these registers are a most useful finding aid for wills and administrations.

The records relating to these taxes were transferred to the PRO by the Inland Revenue and have the lettercode IR. Class IR 27 contains the indexes and class IR 26 the death duty registers. IR 27 is on microfilm and, up to 1858, IR 26 also and so these can be read in the central London reading room as well as at Kew. The registers for 1858-1903 are not filmed and so must be read at Kew. They are stored on another site so at least five working days notice must be given. Death duty registers have not survived for the years after 1903.

These registers may also contain useful genealogical information not given in the will. For example, the names of the children of John Weedon (see chapter 7) were given in the death duty entry, but not in the will. You may also discover the relationship of the beneficiaries to the testator. In the case of administrations they will almost certainly give more information than that given in the act book.

8.1 How to find a death duty register entry

The indexes to the registers are in class IR 27 and the registers themselves in IR 26.

Start with the class list to IR 27. At some dates there are separate lists for the PCC and for the other so-called 'country' courts. The intestates were always indexed separately from those who left wills, so look carefully at the heading at the top of the page of the class list, and not just at the date you want. You will then find the piece number you need, according to the initial letter of the surname, and can help yourself to the appropriate film.

IR 27	Date	Description
		Prerogative Court of Canterbury and Country Courts (contd.)
		Wills
190	1824	K - R
191	1824	S - Z
192	1825	A - D
193	1825	E - J

Suppose you were looking for a death duty entry for George Shore who died in 1824. Here is part of the IR 27 class list. You will see that for a surname beginning with S you will need to take the film of IR 27/191. You will there find:

This shows that the entry for George Shore will be found on folio 339 of the register in IR 26. The second column in the IR 27 entry shown above gives the name and address of one of the executors, and the third column the court of probate. This is probably easier to read in the actual entry in IR 26.

Now go to the IR 26 class lists to convert this reference into an IR 26 volume number. Again make sure you are looking in the section for wills.

I.R.26			Will Registers - Contd.
1016	"	"	1299 - 1665
1017	"	S - T	1 - 343
1018	"	"	345 - 560
1019	"	"	561 - 775

This tells you that the film you need is IR 26/1017. You can see that folio 339 will be towards the end of piece number 1017. This folio is reproduced on pages 46-47.

When looking for a folio number in IR 26 it is important to remember that in this case you are looking for a hand-written number in the top <u>left hand</u> corner of the <u>left hand</u> page. Readers used to looking for wills may find this hard to get used to! Ignore the stamped numbers unless you want to order a photocopy, and then follow the instructions on the back of the order form.

Each entry in an IR 26 register is spread across two pages and in some films these pages appear one on top of the other, as they do in this example, so it is worth ordering photocopies which you can place side by side. One of the top columns on the right hand page tells you where and when the will was proved, in this case the Consistorial Archidiaconal Court of Wells (usually known as the Archdeaconry Court of Wells), on 23 February 1824.

When you have found the court where the will was proved, you can discover the present whereabouts of its records by consulting the FFHS booklet *Probate Jurisdictions: Where to look for wills* which is available in the reading room as well as on sale. Details are given in the bibliography.

Some help in the interpretation of the registers is given in the introductory note to the IR 26 class list and in information leaflets in the reading room.

You can see from this example that although the personal estate of George Shore was valued at 'under £100', at this date (1824), it was subject to tax.

This example has been greatly reduced. If you obtain a photocopy it will be A3, and you can of course read it at a larger magnification on film. Here the stamped number on the right hand page is the same as the manuscript folio number on the left hand page, but usually they are quite different.

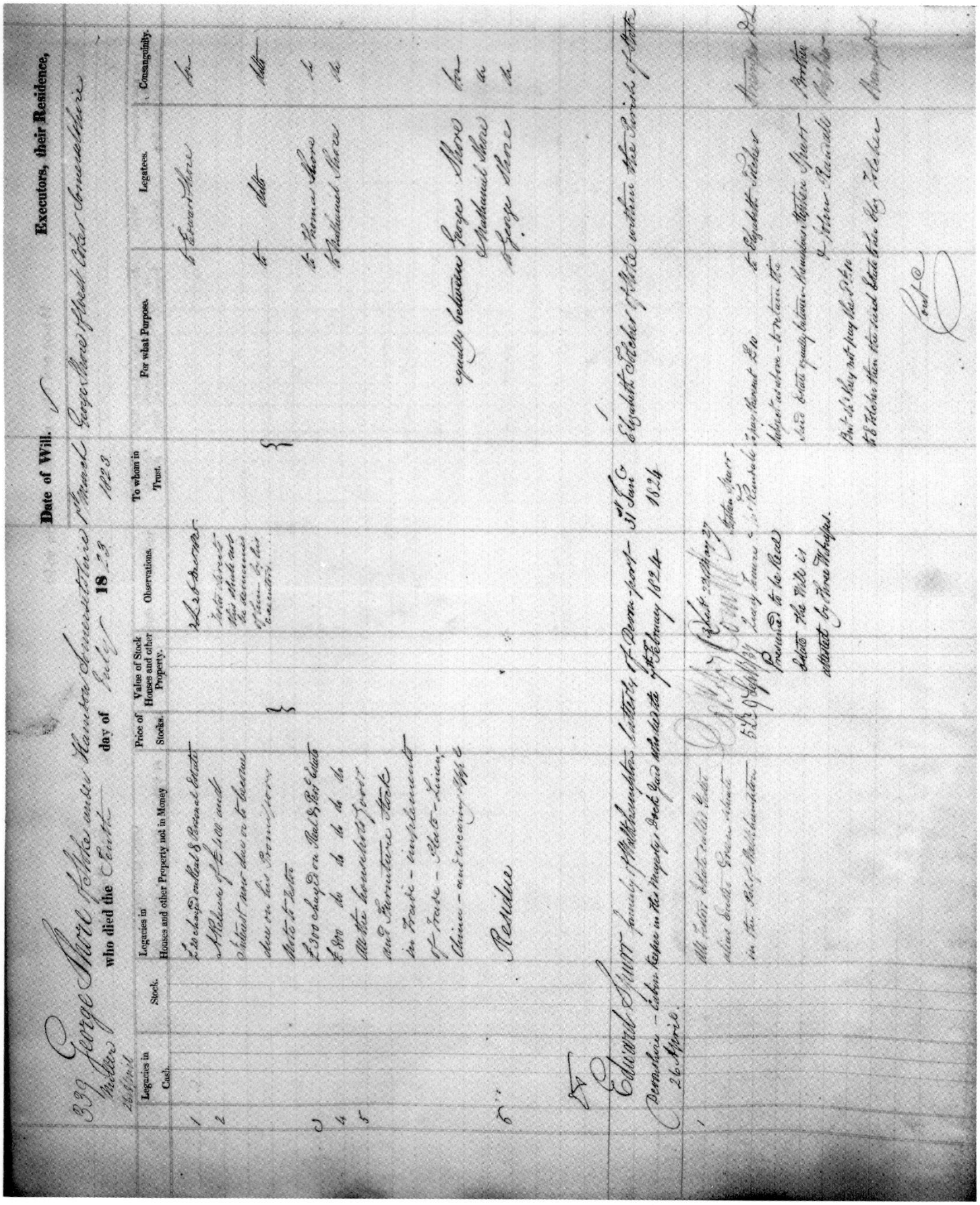
who died the … day of … 18

Date of Will.

Executors, their Residence,

Legacies in Cash.	Stock.	Legacies in Houses and other Property not in Money	Price of Stocks.	Value of Stock Houses and other Property.	Observations.	To whom in Trust.	For what Purpose.	Legatees.	Consanguinity.

Fig 13 An Example of a death duty register entry. IR 26/1017, f 339.

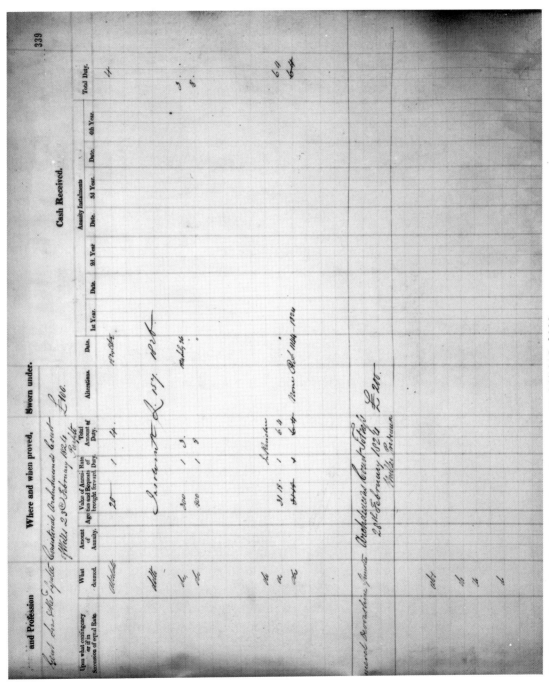

Fig 13 An Example of a death duty register entry. IR 26/1017, f 339.

9. A note on Probate Inventories

A full treatment of this subject is beyond the scope of this book, and in any case a great deal has been published on the subject of which a small sample is given in the bibliography. This chapter will merely indicate how probate inventories may be found among the PCC records and give one complete example with a transcription. Remember that the inventory did not include land: it was a list of moveable goods, and whereas it included credits it did not include debts (see glossary under *Inventory*).

There is, in fact, a relatively small number of PCC inventories, and comparatively few from before 1660 or after the end of the seventeenth century. Many were lost in the Interregnum, and the court ceased to call for them as a matter of course in the eighteenth century.

Appendix D shows you the main PROB classes (PROB 2-PROB 5, PROB 31, PROB 32) which contain inventories, and the dates these classes cover. The inventories have not been filmed, so you will have to read them at Kew. Most have been indexed, some classes on card indexes (kept at Kew) and some in typescript indexes filed with the class lists.

The example given on pages 50-53 (PROB 31/184/20) records the goods and chattels of Ezekiel Pope, a yeoman of Toller Whelme in the parish of Corscombe in Dorset, one of my 5 x great-grandfathers. I found it almost by chance one day when standing beside the PROB 31 card index while waiting for a document.

It is a good example of the way a picture of a house, in this case a farmstead, and its activities may be gained from such a document. It goes through the rooms one by one, and then into the farmyard, barn, pigsty and fields. In this case the inventory was taken only fifteen days after the death of the inhabitant.

Downstairs there is a hall, buttery, kitchen and ?storehouse; upstairs the chamber over the kitchen, the chamber over the hall and the side chamber. (One bedroom contained about one and a half hundredweights of cheeses, and another forty-one cheeses!) I was puzzled at first by the 'reeks' but then the mention of 'hay reeks' made it clear! It may be helpful to read puzzling words aloud as the inventories were often compiled by reliable neighbours, the 'appraisers', who may have spelt phonetically and used local words. The great advantage is that inventories were almost always written in English, even before 1733.

If the construction of a hypothetical picture or plan of a house from an inventory interests you, you will find several examples in John West's *Village Records*. Details and page numbers are given in the bibliography.

A true and perfect Inventory of all and singular
the Goods Chattles and Creditts of Ezekiel Pope late of Toller
Wilm within the parish of Corscombe in the County of
Dorset Yeoman deceased (which since his death have come
to the hands possession or knowledge of John Allen the
Administrator with the Will Annexed of the said deceased)
Taken and Appraised the nine and twentieth day of
October in the year of our Lord one Thousand seven
hundred and thirty five By Robert Richards of Beamister
in the said County of Dorset Malster and James Bagg of
Beamister aforesaid Yeoman whose names are hereunder subscribed.

	£ s d
First his wearing Apparel	02 00 00
In the Hall of his late dwelling house	
One Round Table board Two joyn stools Ten Chairs	
Three Tubbs and One Glass cage	01 02 00
And one Clock with the Case and Wights	01 10 00
In the Buttry	
Eight Barrells one salting-try six Chees Vates	
A Parcell of Milk pans and other small things	01 06 00
In the Kitchin	
Four Brass kittles one Brass pan one Boyler	
Two Brass skillets One Bell Meatle Skillet	
four Brass or Bell Meatle Crocks	02 16 00
Nine pewter platers six pewter plates one	
pewter Tankard and one pewter porrenger	01 04 00
Two Brass Candlesticks One Warming pan Two	
Brass Ladles one Brass pistle and Morter	
and Two Iron Candlesticks	00 07 00
One Table board frame and furm one Gibb four	
Tubbs Six payls one Butter Churn Three Chairs	00 15 00
Pott Crocks Fire dogs firepan and Tongs	
and some other small things	00 03 00
In the stanehouse [?storehouse]	
One Cheesepress Three Wash Tubbs one shovell	
and Two Old sives	00 06 00
In the Kitchin Chamber	
One Feather bed Curtens and Vallens one	
Green Rugg one pair of blankets one sheet	
one feather bolster and one feather pillow	04 00 00
Two halfhead Bedsteads two dustbeds Two	
Ruggs Two blanketts Two sheets one feather	
bolster and one dust Bolster	02 00 00
One Arm Chair and about one hundred	
and half Weight of Cheeses	01 07 00
Table Linnen and other linnen	
Four sheets and other Linnen	00 16 00
Two Coffers Three boxes and some other small things	00 05 00
In the Hall Chamber	
One and Forty Cheeses	01 10 00
Money due for Wool Sold	01 16 00

A true and perfect Inventory of all and singular the Goods Chattles and Credits of [...] late of [...] within the parish of [...] in the County of Dorset Yeoman deceased [...] since his death [...] the [...] possession or knowledge of John [...] Administrator with the will Annexed of the said [...] taken and Appraised the Nine and twentieth day of October in the year of our Lord One thousand Seven Hundred and thirty five By Robert Richards of [...] in the said County of Dorset Maltster and James Bagg of [...] aforesaid Yeoman whose names are hereunder [...]

	l	s	d
First his wearing Apparrell	02	00	00

In the Hall or his last Dwelling house

One Round Table board two joynt stools two Chairs
three Dishes and one Glasscage
And one Clock with the Case and weights — 01 10 00 (02 00)

In the Buttry
Eight Barrells one Salting ky six three barrells
A parrell of Milk pans and other small things — 01 05 00

In the Kitchin
Four Brass Kittles one Brass pan One Boyler
Two Brass Skillets one [...] meate Skillet — 02 16 00
four Brass or Brass [...] Corbs
Nine Pewter platers six pewter plates one [...]
[...] two brass Candlesticks one warming pan [...]
Brass ladles one Brass pestle and morter — 07 00
and two Iron Candle Sticks
One table board frame and form one Gill four
[...] six payls one butter Churn three Chairs — 00 15 00
Pott Crocks Fire dogs fire pan and tongs — 00 03 00
And some other small things

In the Store house
One Cheese press three [...] tubs one [...] — 00 06 00
and two old [...]

In the Kitchin Chamber
One feather bed Curtains and Vallens one
Green Rugg one pair of blankets one Sheet — 04 00 00
one feather bolster and one feather pillows
Two half head steads two dust beds two
Ruggs two Blankets two Sheets one feather — 02 00 00
bolster and one dust bolster
One Arm Chair and about one Hundred — 01 07 00
and half weight of Cheese

Table linnen and other linnen
ffour Sheets and other linnen — 00 16 00
Two Coffers three boxes and some other small things — 00 05 00

In the Hall Chamber
One and forty Cheeses — 01 10 00
[...] — 01 16 00

Fig 14
An example of a probate inventory PROB 31/184/20.

51

	£ s d
One halfhead Bedstead one quarter Barrell	
a pair of Weights and Weight stores and old dust beds	00 10 00
And about Ten Weight of Wooll	08 00 00
In the side Chamber	
Some old Iron and five Boards	00 04 00
In the Barn and Reek barton	
For Wheat Beans and Oats therein and	
Two Reeks in the said Barton	08 00 00
In the Pigsty	
One fatt Pigg	01 10 00
In the Feilds	
One and Fifty sheep	22 00 00
One and Twenty Hog-Sheep	04 00 00
six Milch Cows	12 00 00
One Gray Mare	02 10 00
Four Hay Reeks	05 00 00
In the Barton and Coppis	
One old Cart and Wheels and some old	
Plough-tackling and Wood	01 00 00
Security for money due	
One surrender by way of Mortgage for securing	
the payment of Eighty pounds and Interest	80 00 00
One Bond for Sixty pounds Conditioned for the	
payment of Thirty pounds and Interest	30 00 00
One other Bond of the penalty of Forty pounds	
whereof fifteen pounds of the said Bond was paid	
the Estate before his death so there is now due	05 00 00
In Ready Money	
Two hundred and sexty seven pounds and	
six shillings	267 06 00
In some old Lumber and things of little Value	00 05 00
	470 08 00

Robt Richards
James Bagg   Appraisors

This Examinant Declares that no
other Goods Chattles or Creditts of
the said deceased have since his
Death come to his hands possession
or knowledge.
John Allen

The one and Twentieth day of
December in the year 1738
The said John Allen was
sworn to the Truth of this Inventory
before me.   Hen: mintern

brought in 17 Jany 1738/9

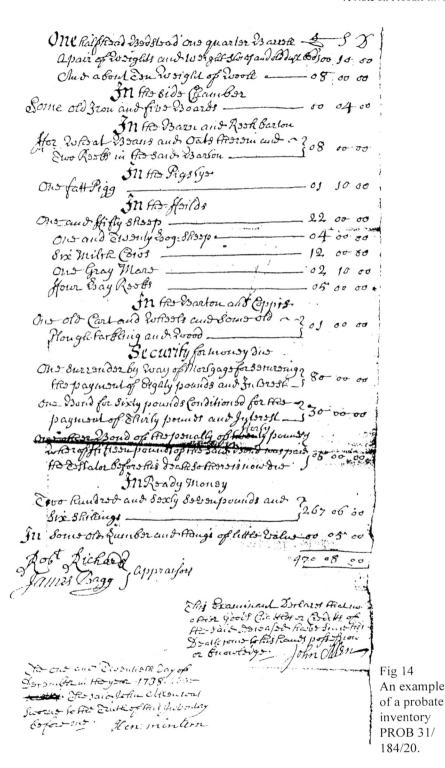

Fig 14
An example
of a probate
inventory
PROB 31/
184/20.

Postscript

The closure of probate business in the PCC is recorded in the last two pages of PROB 11 (PROB 11/2263, f 24A).

By... An Act to amend the Law relating to Probates and Letters of Administration in England

> it is enacted that the voluntary and contentious Jurisdiction and Authority of All Ecclesiastical, Royal Peculiar, Peculiar, Manorial and other Courts and Persons in England now having Jurisdiction or Authority to grant or revoke Probate of Wills or Letters of Administration of the Effects of deceased Persons, shall in respect of such Matters absolutely cease...
> The voluntary and contentious Jurisdiction and authority...shall belong to and be vested in Her Majesty and shall...be exercised in the Name of Her Majesty in a Court to be called the Court of Probate...
>
> At the Court at Buckingham Palace the 2nd day of December, 1857...
>
> Her Majesty...is pleased to Order and appoint...that the said recited Act... shall come into operation on the Eleventh day of January next... and that the above mentioned Court of Probate shall hold its ordinary sittings in any of the Courts in Westminster Hall which can be conveniently used for the purpose and shall have its Principal Registry in the City of London in the building now used as the public Registry of the Prerogative Court of the Archbishop of Canterbury.

These days, however, wills proved and administrations granted after 11 January 1858 are to be found in the Principal Registry of the Family Division of the High Court of Justice, at present in Somerset House; or the local district registries or record offices listed on page 11 of the FFHS booklet *Probate Jurisdictions* (see bibliography).

Appendix A: SEATS OF THE PCC 1719-1858

(see chapter 1.3, page 9).

1. **Registrar's Seat**
a) Testators or intestates dying overseas or at sea, except in cases where the grant was made to the widow of the deceased and she lived within the province of Canterbury, in which case probate or administration was granted in the appropriate seat.
b) Testators or intestates living outside the province of Canterbury.
c) Estates which were, had been or might be subject to litigation within the PCC. If, however, a subsequent grant was made it would be passed at the seat that would have been responsible had there been no litigation.

The range of cases dealt with by the Registrar's seat is illustrated by the page from PROB 6 reproduced as page 13.

2. Surrey Seat
Cornwall
Devon
Dorset
Hampshire
Somerset
Surrey
Sussex
Wiltshire

3. Welsh Seat
Berkshire
Derbyshire
Gloucestershire
Herefordshire
Leicestershire
Northamptonshire
Oxfordshire
Rutland
Shropshire
Staffordshire
Warwickshire
Worcestershire
Wales

4. Middlesex Seat
Bedfordshire
Buckinghamshire
Cambridgeshire
Essex
Hertfordshire
Huntingdonshire
Kent
Lincolnshire
Middlesex (excluding those parishes and other administrative areas within the county subject to the London seat)
Norfolk
Suffolk

5. London Seat
City of London
Some parishes and other administrative areas in Middlesex (or partly in Middlesex and partly in the City of London)

The English counties listed here, together with Wales, comprised the ecclesiastical province of Canterbury. All other English counties are in the province of York.

There are lists of the Middlesex parishes subject to the London seat in the appendixes to the introductory notes to PROB 46 and PROB 52.

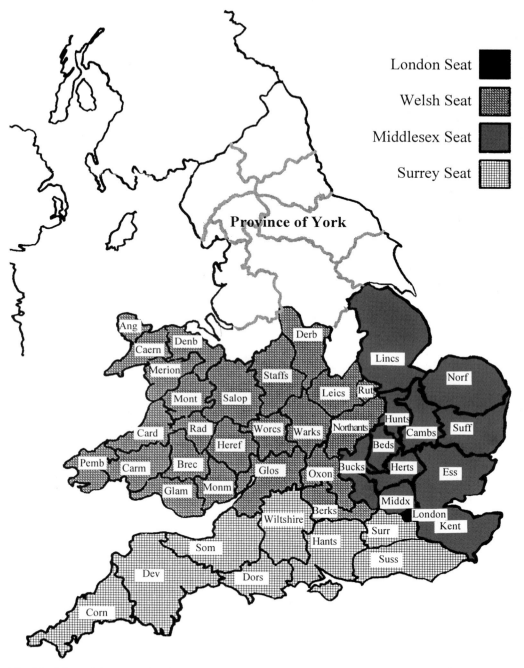

London Seat

Welsh Seat

Middlesex Seat

Surrey Seat

Province of York

Ang
Caern
Denb
Merion
Mont
Salop
Staffs
Derb
Lincs
Norf
Card
Rad
Worcs
Warks
Leics
Rut
Hunts
Cambs
Suff
Pemb
Carm
Brec
Heref
Northants
Beds
Herts
Ess
Glam
Monm
Glos
Oxon
Bucks
Middx
London
Kent
Wiltshire
Berks
Surr
Som
Hants
Suss
Dev
Dors
Corn

Fig 15   Map of the ecclesiastical province of Canterbury, showing division into seats by the PCC.

Some Middlesex parishes and administrative areas were subject to the Middlesex seat, others were subject to the London seat. See page 55.

Fig 16   Graph showing distribution by county of the PCC wills and administrations, 1730.

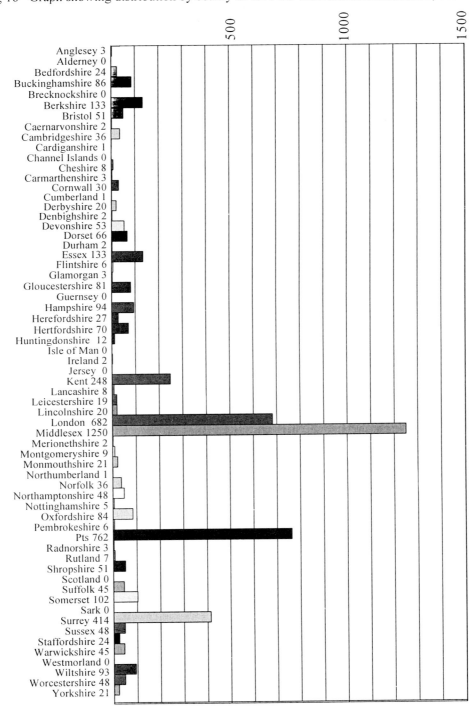

Appendix B: Indexes to PCC wills and administrations

A   Wills, probate acts, 1383-1700

A1	1383-1558	*Index of wills proved in the Prerogative Court of Canterbury*, [vol I A-J, vol II K-Z], compiled by J Challenor C Smith, Index Library, X-XI (London, British Record Society, 1893-1895).
A2	1558-1583	*ibid*, vol III, compiled by S A Smith and edited by Leland L Duncan, Index Library, XVIII (London, British Record Society, 1898).
A3	1584-1604	*ibid*, vol IV, compiled by S A Smith and edited by Edward Alexander Fry, Index Library, XXV (London, British Record Society, 1901).
A4	1605-1619	*ibid*, vol V, compiled by E Stokes, Index Library, XLIII (London, British Record Society, 1912).
A5	1620-1629	*ibid*, vol VI, edited by R H Ernest Hill, Index Library, XLIV (London, British Record Society, 1912).
A6	1620-1624	*Year book of probates: Abstracts of probates and sentences in the Prerogative Court of Canterbury*, edited by John Matthews and George F Matthews (London, 1914). This index contains some references not in A5. The abbreviations it uses are explained in A7.1, p. 5. It does not have a place name index, but there is one in A5.
A7		*Year books of probates (from 1630): Abstracts of probate acts in the Prerogative Court of Canterbury*, edited by John Matthews and George F Matthews (London, 1902-1927).
A7.1	1630-1634	vol I (1902).
A7.2	1635-1639	vol II (1903).
A7.3	1630-1639	*Sentences and complete index nominum (probates and sentences)*. Extra volume (1907). This volume indexes sentences 1630-1639, and all surnames in it and in A7.1-2.

A7.4	1640-1644	vol III (1905).
A7.5	1645-1649	vol IV (1906).
		Tracing wills and probate acts 1643-1646 is subject to particular difficulties. Further information is supplied in the introductory notes to the PROB 8 and PROB 10 class lists.
A7.6	1650-1651	vol V (1909).
A7.7	1652-1653	vol VI (1911).
A7.8	1654	vol VII (1914).
A7.9	1655	vol VIII [Surnames A-Musgrave only] (1927).

A7.8-9 do not have place name indexes, but there is one in A8 which covers the same period.

A8	1653-1656	*Index of wills proved in the Prerogative Court of Canterbury*, vol VII, edited by Thomas M Blagg and Josephine Skeate Moir, Index Library, LIV (London, British Record Society, 1925).
A9	1657-1660	*ibid*, vol VIII, edited by Thomas M Blagg, Index Library, LXI (London, British Record Society, 1936).
A10	1661-1670	*Prerogative Court of Canterbury: Wills, sentences and probate acts*, edited by J H Morrison (London, 1935).
A11	1671-1675	*Index of wills proved in the Prerogative Court of Canterbury*, vol IX, edited by John Ainsworth, Index Library, LXVII (London, British Record Society, 1942).
A12	1676-1685	*ibid*, vol X, edited by C Harold Ridge, Index Library, LXXI (London, British Record Society, 1948).
A13	1686-1693	*ibid*, vol XI, edited by C Harold Ridge, Index Library, LXXVII (London, British Record Society, 1958).
A14	1694-1700	*ibid*, vol XII, edited by Marc Fitch, Index Library, LXXX (London, British Record Society, 1960).

B Administration acts 1559-1700

B1	1559-1571	*Administrations in the Prerogative Court of Canterbury*, [vol I], edited by Reginald M Glencross (Exeter, 1912).
B2	1572-1580	*ibid*, vol II (Exeter, 1917).

B3	1559-1580	Beric Lloyd, Preliminary addenda and corrigenda to Mr R M Glencross's letters of administration granted by the Prerogative Court of Canterbury, 1559-1580 (typescript, 1979).
B4	1581-1595	*Index to administrations in the Prerogative Court of Canterbury*, vol III, edited by C Harold Ridge, Index Library, LXXVI (London, British Record Society, 1954).
B5	1596-1608	*ibid*, vol IV, edited by Marc Fitch, Index Library, LXXXI (London, British Record Society, 1964).
B6	1609-1619	*ibid*, vol V, edited by Marc Fitch, Index Library, LXXXIII (London, British Record Society, 1968).
B7	1620-1630	*Prerogative Court of Canterbury: Letters of administration*, edited by J H Morrison (London, 1935).
B8	1631-1648	*ibid*, vol VI, edited by Marc Fitch, Index Library, C (London, British Record Society, 1986).
B9	1643-1644	Grants made at Oxford, registered in PROB 6/234, and omitted from B8. A contemporary index of intestates in PROB 6/234 has been reproduced and is available on the open shelves. This index was formerly PROB 12/23B.
B10	1649-1654	*Index to administrations in the Prerogative Court of Canterbury*, vol I, edited by John Ainsworth, Index Library, LXVIII (London, British Record Society, 1944).
B11	1655-1660	*ibid*, vol II, edited by C Harold Ridge, 3 vols, Index Library, LXXII (A-F), LXXIV (G-Q), LXXV (R-Z) (London, British Record Society, 1949-1953).
B12	1661	Surnames A - Sweetinge: Index to PROB 6/37 (typescript).
B13	1661	Surnames other than those in the sequence A - Sweetinge: PROB 12/38.
B14	1662	PROB 12/39. The administration act book for 1662 is not extant.
B15	1663-1664	Index to PROB 6/38-39 (typescript).

B16   1665-1700   PROB 12/41-69.

C   Wills, probate acts, and administration acts 1701-1858

C1   1701-1749   See page 20.

C2   1750-1800   Wills: *An index to wills proved in the Prerogative Court of Canterbury 1750-1800*, edited by Anthony J Camp, vol I, A-Bh (1976); vol II, Bi-Ce (1977); vol III, Ch-G (1984); vol IV, H-M (1988); vol V, N-Sh (1991); vol VI, Si-Z (1992) (London, Society of Genealogists).

C3   1750-1800   Administrations: PROB 12/120-176.
(There is a card index to administrations 1750-1800 compiled from PROB 13/186-236 at the Society of Genealogists, which is being prepared for publication. The Society will search it for a fee. The Society's address is 14 Charterhouse Buildings, Goswell Road, London EC1 7BA). See page 21.

C4   1801-1852   PROB 12/177-271.
A partial printed source of information on PCC wills proved in the period 1807 to 1845 is *An index to the Bank of England will extracts, 1807-1845*, Society of Genealogists (1991). If the name of a testator appears in this index it is very likely that his or her will was proved in the PCC. This index relates only to testators who bequeathed Bank of England stock in their wills and therefore excludes many testators. As a printed source it has the advantage of being available outside the PRO.

C5   1853-1858   *Calendar of the grants of probate and letters of administration made in the Prerogative Court of Canterbury 1853-1857, 1858*, 16 vols. (London, nd). PROB 12/272-288. (Locations of copies of this index outside the PRO are listed in Jeremy Gibson, *Probate jurisdictions: where to look for wills*, fourth edition (Solihull, 1994), p. 2. The index has also been published in microfiche by the Hampshire Record Office, together with the calendars of grants of probate and administration for 1858 to 1935.)

D American probate and administration acts 1610 to 1857

Peter Wilson Coldham, *American wills and administrations in the Prerogative Court of Canterbury, 1610-1857* (Baltimore, 1989). This work supersedes Coldham's earlier works on the same subject. It can be used to advantage in conjunction with his *American wills proved in London, 1611-1775* (Baltimore, 1992).

E Other indexes

Other indexes, for example to individual counties, are listed in the FFHS booklet *Probate Jurisdictions* (see bibliography).

Appendix C: Alphabetical list of names of registers

Until 1840, the will register for each year was given a name, after the name of a prominent person whose will was contained in it. See page 16 for further information.

Abbott, 1729
Abercrombie, 1801
Adderley, 1800
Adeane, 1506
Alchin, 1654
Alen, 1546
Alenger, 1540
Alexander, 1775
Anstis, 1744
Arden, 1840
Arran, 1759
Arundell, 1580
Ash, 1704
Aston, 1714
Auber, 1730
Audley, 1632
Aylett, 1655
Ayloffe, 1517

Babington, 1568
Bakon, 1579
Bargrave, 1774
Barnes, 1712
Barrett, 1708
Barrington, 1628
Bath, 1680
Beard, 1830
Bedford, 1732
Bellas, 1776
Bence, 1676
Bennett, 1508
Berkley, 1656
Bettesworth, 1752
Bevor, 1791
Bishop, 1790
Blamyr, 1501
Bodfelde, 1523
Bogg, 1769
Bolein, 1603
Bolton, 1724
Bond, 1696
Bowyer, 1652
Box, 1694
Boycott, 1743
Brent, 1653
Bridport, 1814
Brodrepp, 1738
Brook, 1728
Browne, 1740
Browning, 1719
Bruce, 1664
Brudenell, 1585
Bucke, 1551
Buckingham, 1721
Bunce, 1674
Busby, 1751
Butts, 1583
Byrde, 1624

Cæsar, 1763
Calvert, 1788
Cambell, 1642
Cann, 1685
Capell, 1613
Carew, 1576
Carr, 1667
Chaynay, 1559
Chayre, 1563
Cheslyn, 1761
Clarke, 1625
Cobham, 1597
Coke, 1669
Coker, 1693
Collier, 1777
Collingwood, 1810
Collins, 1780
Coode, 1550
Cope, 1616
Cornwallis, 1783
Cottle, 1682
Coventry, 1640
Crane, 1643
Cresswell, 1818
Crickitt, 1811
Crumwell, 1536
Crymes, 1565

Dale, 1621
Daper, 1572
Darcy, 1581
Daughtry, 1577
Degg, 1703
Derby, 1736
Dixy, 1594
Dodwell, 1793
Dogett, 1491
Dorset, 1609
Drake, 1596
Drax, 1683
Drury, 1590
Ducarel, 1785
Ducie, 1735
Duke, 1671
Dycer, 1675
Dyer, 1701
Dyke, 1690
Dyngeley, 1537

Edmunds, 1746
Eedes, 1706
Effingham, 1817
Ellenboro', 1819
Ely, 1808
Ent, 1689
Erskine, 1824
Essex, 1648

Eure, 1672
Evelyn, 1641
Exeter, 1797
Exton, 1688

Fagg, 1715
Fairfax, 1649
Fane, 1692
Farquhar, 1833
Farrant, 1727
Fenner, 1612
Fetiplace, 1511
Fines, 1647
Foot, 1687
Fountain, 1792
Fox, 1716

Gee, 1705
Glazier, 1756
Gloucester, 1835
Goare, 1637
Godyn, 1463
Gostling, 1782
Greenly, 1750
Grey, 1651

Hale, 1677
Hare, 1684
Harrington, 1592
Harris, 1796
Harte, 1604
Harvey, 1639
Hay, 1778
Hayes, 1605
Heathfield, 1813
Heber, 1827
Hele, 1626
Henchman, 1739
Hene, 1668
Herne, 1702
Herring, 1757
Herschell, 1822
Heseltine, 1804
Hogen, 1533
Holder, 1514
Holgrave, 1504
Holman, 1794
Holney, 1571
Horne, 1496
Howe, 1799
Hudleston, 1607
Hutton, 1758
Hyde, 1665
Irby, 1695
Isham, 1731
Jankyn, 1529
Jenner, 1770
Juxon, 1663

Kent, 1820
Kenyon, 1802
Ketchyn, 1556
Kidd, 1599
King, 1679

Lane, 1709
Langley, 1578
Laud, 1662
Lawe, 1614
Lee, 1638
Leeds, 1713
Legard, 1767
Leicester, 1588
Lewyn, 1597
Lisle, 1749
Liverpool, 1829
Lloyd, 1686
Loftes, 1561
Logge, 1479
Lort, 1698
Loveday, 1809
Luffenam, 1423
Lushington, 1807
Lynch, 1760
Lyon, 1570

Macham, 1789
Major, 1787
Mansfield, 1821
Marche, 1401
Marlbro', 1722
Marriott, 1803
Martyn, 1574
May, 1661
Maynwaryng, 1520
Meade, 1618
Mellershe, 1559
Mico, 1666
Milles, 1487
Montague, 1602
Moone, 1500
More, 1554
Morrison & Crymes, 1565

Nabbs, 1660
Nelson, 1805
Nevell, 1593
Newcastle, 1795
Nicholl, 1838
Noel, 1700
Noodes, 1558
Norfolk, 1786
North, 1681
Norwich, 1837

Ockham, 1734
Oxford, 1812

Pakenham, 1815
Parker, 1619
Paul, 1755
Pell, 1659
Pembroke, 1650
Penn, 1670
Peter, 1573
Pett, 1699
Pile, 1636
Pinfold, 1754
Pitt, 1806
Plymouth, 1726
Poley, 1707
Populwell, 1548
Porch, 1525
Potter, 1747
Powell, 1552
Price, 1733
Pyckering, 1575
Pye, 1673
Pyne, 1697
Pynnyng, 1544

Reeve, 1678
Richards, 1823
Richmond, 1723
Ridley, 1629
Rivers, 1644
Rockingham, 1784
Romney, 1725
Rous, 1384
Rowe, 1583
Rudd, 1615
Rushworth, 1765
Russell, 1633
Ruthen, 1657
Rutland, 1588

Sadler, 1635
Sainberbe, 1591
St. Albans, 1825
St. Eloy, 1762
St. John, 1631
Savile, 1622
Scott, 1595
Scroope, 1630
Seager, 1634
Searle, 1753
Secker, 1768
Seymer, 1745
Shaller, 1720
Sheffelde, 1569
Simpson, 1764

Skinner, 1627
Smith, 1710
Soame, 1620
Spencer, 1587
Spert, 1541
Spurway, 1741
Stafford, 1606
Stevens, 1773
Stevenson, 1564
Stokton, 1454
Stonard, 1567
Stowell, 1836
Strahan, 1748
Streat, 1562
Sutton, 1828
Swabey, 1826
Swann, 1623

Tashe, 1553
Taverner, 1772
Tebbs, 1831
Teignmouth, 1834
Tenterden, 1832
Tenison, 1718
Thower, 1531
Tirwhite, 1582
Trenley, 1742
Trevor, 1771
Twisse, 1646
Tyndall, 1766

Vaughan, 1839
Vere, 1691
Vox, 1493

Wake, 1737
Wallop, 1600
Walpole, 1798
Warburton, 1779
Watson, 1584
Wattys, 1471
Webster, 1781
Weldon, 1617
Welles, 1558
Whitfield, 1717
Windebanck, 1608
Windsor, 1586
Wingfield, 1610
Wood, 1611
Woodhall, 1601
Wootton, 1658
Wrastley, 1557
Wynne, 1816

Young, 1711

Appendix D: Selected PROB classes

All these classes are kept at Kew, but those which have been filmed (PROB 6 and PROB 11) can also be read in the PRO's central London reading room.

PROB 1   Original wills of some famous people.

PROB 2   Inventories, 1417-1660. The few PCC inventories that have survived from this period are largely in this class. There are indexes of persons, locations and occupations. See chapter 9.

PROB 3   Inventories, 1702, 1718-1782. There are indexes of persons and places. Other inventories for this period are to be found in: PROB 4, PROB 5, PROB 31. See chapter 9.

PROB 4   Inventories exhibited post 1660. A list and card indexes of surnames and places are available. See chapter 9.

PROB 5   Inventories and accounts mostly produced as a result of litigation. The majority date from 1667-1722. There is a list and personal name index. See chapter 9.

PROB 6   Administration act books 1559-1858. Registers of grants made in cases of intestacy. See chapter 1, section 3. This class is produced to readers on microfilm and can be read in the PRO's central London reading room as well as at Kew.

PROB 7   Limited and special administrations 1810-1858. Until 1810 these will be found in PROB 6. After that date if a note is found in PROB 6 that an administration is 'E.A.L.' it will be found 'entered at length' in PROB 7. See chapter 1.6.

PROB 8   Probate act books 1526-1858. Registers of grants of probate. See chapter 4.

PROB 9   Limited and special probates 1781, 1800, 1802-1804, 1806-1858. At those dates if a note is found in PROB 8 that a grant of probate is 'E.A.L.' it is 'entered at length' in PROB 9. At other dates it will be found in PROB 8. See chapter 1.5.

PROB 10   Original wills 1383-1858. See chapter 5.

PROB 11   Registered copy wills 1383-1858. Volumes containing parchment copies of almost all the wills proved in the PCC. See chapter 1, section 2. They are produced to readers on microfilm and can be read in the central London reading room

PROB 12   Indexes to wills and administrations 1383-1858. See chapter 1, sections 1 and 4.

PROB 18   Allegations 1661-1858. In cases of litigation, the plaintiff made an allegation to which the defendant made an answer (which will be found, if it survives, in PROB 25 or PROB 28). There is a card index to PROB 18. See chapter 6. Allegations will also be found in classes PROB 28, PROB 31 and PROB 37.

PROB 24   Depositions 1657-1809. The evidence taken from witnesses who 'appeared personally' before officials of the PCC in London. The evidence taken locally, 'by commission', is in PROB 28. Most of the volumes have integral indexes by plaintiff.

PROB 25   Answers 1664-1854. The answer was the response made by the defendant to the plaintiff's allegation. See chapter 6.

PROB 26   Depositions bound by suit 1826-1857. By the 1820s the evidence taken in long and complicated cases could be very bulky, and was often bound in volumes and kept separately from other depositions in PROB 31. There are indexes by deceased and plaintiff.

PROB 28   Cause papers, early series, 1642-1722. The depositions of witnesses, answers of defendants and affidavits taken by commission were kept in this series, separate from the evidence and pleadings submitted personally in London.

PROB 29   Act of court books, contested causes, 1536-1819. These volumes contain minutes of the court's proceedings in contentious testamentary business, but it is procedural detail which is recorded: there is little detail about the matter of the litigation. Renunciations by executors and administrators and the appointment of guardians for minors are also recorded. After 1819 use PROB 30.

PROB 30   Acts of court 1740-1858. The original acts from which PROB 29 was compiled. They are arranged in monthly bundles, roughly alphabetically by the name of the deceased.

PROB 31   Exhibits, main series, 1722-1858. This class includes a variety of documents such as proxies, affidavits, commissions, elections of guardians for minors, inventories, wills, codicils and other testamentary papers. There is on the shelves an index to wills in this class and also a card index (of names and places) of the inventories in this class and to those few in PROB 37. The index to the whole class is in PROB 33. For help with using this class, see chapter 6.

PROB 32   Files of exhibits 1661-1723. The majority are inventories and they relate mainly to London and Middlesex. List and index available. See chapter 9.

PROB 33   Indexes to exhibits, 1722-1858. There are photocopies of these volumes on the shelves. The documents to which they refer are in classes PROB 26, PROB 31, PROB 37, and various other classes. For help with using this class, see chapter 6.

PROB 37   Cause papers, later series, 1783-1858. Towards the end of the eighteenth century the registry clerks of the PCC started removing the larger bundles of depositions taken by commission from the main series of exhibits (now PROB 31) and keeping them separately. Gradually other exhibits were added to them and they now constitute the class PROB 37. There is a detailed list and index. See chapter 6.2.

These classes have been selected as those most likely to be of use to readers looking for biographical or genealogical information. The remaining classes are likely to be of interest largely to those concerned with judicial process or with the internal administration of the PCC.

There is a full list of every PRO class, including all PROB classes, in part 2 of the PRO *Current guide* of which there is a copy in every reading room. You will find fuller accounts of the classes in the introductory notes that preface the class lists.

Appendix E: Alphabet

of the script used in PROB 11 in the nineteenth century, which had evolved gradually during the eighteenth century.

In each case the example of the small letter is underlined.

Allington Catharine	Nuttolls Henry
Bayles Elizabeth	Owen Nicholas
Colman Richard	Plummer Penelope
Dennis Edward	Quartermaine Jaquil
Efton James	Rudyard Richard
Hansfield Thomas	Storrus Charles
Baring George	Tindall Stephen
Hill John	Urwin Samuel
Irwin Thomas	Vavasor Catherine
Jones Benjamin	Wollsser Lawrence
Kirkham Mary	Ximenes Alexander
Ludlam Richard	Yelverton Mary
Matson James	Zouch Elizabeth

Abbreviations and Glossary

A	Administration.
Account	In probate records, usually refers to an account of administration or executorship, giving details of the distribution of the personal estate and of the administrator's or executor's expenses. Accounts are to be found in PROB 2-PROB 5, PROB 31, PROB 32 and PROB 37.
Act book	The books which record the orders of the court. The granting of probate to an executor is recorded in the probate act books in class PROB 8 (see chapter 4) and the grants of administration in the administration act books in class PROB 6 (see chapter 1.3).
Administration	A grant giving the right to administer, in accordance with certain legal requirements, an estate, usually that of a person who died intestate, that is, leaving no valid will. An administrator might also be appointed where an executor of a will was a minor or where there was no competent executor. See chapters 1.3 and 2.1.2.
Administration (with the will annexed)	A grant by the probate court to the next-of-kin (or some other person or persons) when the will did not specify any executors or they were unable to act, or had renounced, or had died. The administrator was then required to administer the estate according to the terms of the will. See chapter 1.2.3.
Administratrix	A woman administrator.
Admon	Administration.
Allegation	The pleading of either party to a lawsuit. See description of class PROB 18 in chapter 6.1.
AW	Administration (with the will annexed).
Bequeath	To leave by will, properly only used for personal property. *Devise* was used for real estate.
Calendar	In a probate court, a list of names of the testators or intestates for whose estates a grant of probate or administration has been made. It may serve as an index to the wills and administrations but is often arranged by initial letter of surname only, and then chronologically.
Codicil	A signed and witnessed addition (similar to a postscript) to the end of a will by the testator after the will had been made and signed.
Commission	A document appointing a person to perform a specified task. Executors and administrators who did not appear personally in the PCC were sworn 'by commission', usually by the local clergyman. The court might

	also appoint by commission officials to do other things, for example take inventories or examine witnesses.
Cousin german	First cousin, that is, the child of an uncle or aunt.
Coverture	Condition of a woman being married and under a husband's protection.
d b n, or de bo non, or similar	Abbreviation of the Latin phrase meaning 'of goods unadministered' in references to earlier grants.
Dec.	Decree.
Decree	A judgment of the court. In the probate calendars in PROB 12 a note may be found *by decree* or *by int. dec.* (interlocutory decree) indicating contested proceedings had taken place prior to the grant of probate. See chapter 6.1.
Depositions	Testimony, usually in writing, given under oath. Sometimes called affidavits.
Devise	To leave by will, properly only applied to real estate, as distinct from personal property where the term *bequeath* is used.
Double probate	If more than one executor was appointed in a will but only one of them initially took the oath as executor, power would be reserved by the court to make later similar grants of probate to the other persons appointed as executors. These subsequent grants of probate were known as double probates, treble probates, etc.
EAL	Entered at length. Special and limited probates and administrations were 'entered at length' in classes PROB 9 and PROB 7. See appendix D.
EIC	East India Company.
Exhibit	Evidence produced in court. See description of class PROB 31 on pages 33-34.
Estate	The collective assets and liabilities of a person, especially of a deceased person.
Executor	A man appointed by a testator to execute his or her will, that is, to dispose of his estate in accordance with the wishes expressed in the will.
Executrix	A woman executor.
FFHS	Federation of Family History Societies.
Folio	A leaf of a book, numbered only on its *recto* (front). A page is one side of a folio. In PCC records and publications about them the term is sometimes used, contrary to normal usage, to refer to a quire of a will register in PROB 11 (see *Quire* below).

FPRO	Friends of the Public Record Office. A registered charity whose volunteers are involved in indexing projects at the PRO. It publishes a journal, *Prophile*, and holds occasional conferences, lectures and workshops.
German	Cousin german. See *Cousin german* above.
Grant	An act transferring power. Hence, for example, the court granted administration of an intestate's estate to the next-of-kin.
Green book	In the nineteenth century, in PROB 12, entries for soldiers and sailors which appear in the lists at the end of the volumes are sometimes referred to as being in 'the Green book' or the green calendar. These volumes are in PROB 15 series IV but contain no additional information to that given in PROB 12. See page 1.
Holograph will	A will written entirely in the handwriting of the person making the will.
Int.Dec.	Interlocutory decree. See *Decree* above.
Intestate	A person who died without making a will or for whom no valid will was found.
Inventory	A probate inventory is a list of personal and household goods, usually including the tools of trade, etc, left by the deceased, with their appraised value. It includes the credits but excludes the debts and liabilities of the deceased, and any real estate. See chapter 9.
LH	Left hand (page). LH and RH (right hand) are used when ordering photocopies of PCC records from film to indicate which page is required.
Limited administrations	Cases where the grant was limited to part of the estate. See chapter 1.6.
Limited probates	Cases where the grant was limited to part of the estate of the testator. See chapter 1.5.
Minor	A person under the age of twenty-one years.
N B	North Britain, ie Scotland.
Nuncupative will	A will made orally by a testator. Witnesses wrote the statements of the testator and were required to swear to the truth of the statements. The majority of nuncupative wills were made by individuals in extremely poor health or those actually at the point of death, especially soldiers and seamen. For an example, see page 23.
PCC	Prerogative Court of Canterbury, the Archbishop's court. The senior probate court of the province of Canterbury (see appendix A).

Personalty	Personal property (goods, chattels, credits, etc) as opposed to real (land) property. The jurisdiction of probate courts was limited to the disposal of personalty.
PRO	The Public Record Office.
PROB	The lettercode or prefix given to all classes of PCC records. It is followed by the class number (eg PROB 11) and then the piece number (eg PROB 11/1933). It is always written entirely in capitals.
Probate	Evidence that a document offered as the last will and testament of the deceased has been accepted by the court and that the executor has been granted permission to carry out the provisions of the will. The term also refers to the process of proving a will.
Proved	A will was proved when it was accepted by the appropriate court as the authentic and duly attested expression of the wishes of the testator.
Province	The area of jurisdiction of an archbishop. See appendix A.
Pts	An abbreviation of the Latin phrase *in partibus transmarinis* (in countries overseas). It might be used instead of a place of residence for people who died abroad or at sea. See appendix A.
Quire	In the PCC, a series of sixteen pages in the will registers in PROB 11. The word is derived from the fact that a set of four sheets of paper or parchment was folded so as to form eight leaves and sixteen pages.
Realty or real property	Property in land (real estate), as opposed to *personalty*.
Registers and registered wills	Volumes containing copies of wills that have been proved. In the PCC they are in class PROB 11 and affidavits connected with the wills are sometimes registered with them.
Relict	(in Latin *relicta* or *relictus*) A person who is left behind after the decease of his or her spouse. Usually relates to the widow.
Renunciation	When a person, who is named as executor in a will, or is the next-of-kin of an intestate, declines to apply for a grant of probate or administration, he or she is said to have renounced, and usually signs a document known as a proxy of renunciation.
RH	Right hand (page). See also LH.
Seat	From 1719 the place of residence of the deceased determined which 'seat', or administrative division of the PCC, dealt with the probate or grant of administration, except in those cases dealt with by the Registrar. See appendix A.

Sen(t).	Sentence.
Sentence	A final judgment, determination and opinion given at the conclusion of litigation, including cases about disputed wills. See chapter 6.2.
Sig	Signature. The term by which quires are referred to in certain PRO references.
Special probate or administration	As with limited probate or administration the powers of the executor or administrator were limited to parts of the estate. See chapter 1.5 and 1.6.
Testament	See *Will*.
Testator	A man who has made his last will and testament.
Testatrix	A woman who has made her last will and testament.
W	Will.
Will	A written statement by which a person regulates the disposition of property and rights after his or her death. *Will* is a general term sometimes referred to as a *last will and testament*. However, anciently a will set out the deceased's wishes in regard to *real* property, whereas a testament applied only to the disposition of *personalty* (which see).

Certain of these definitions are derived from Gardner and Smith (see bibliography).

Short Bibliography

Guides to probate jurisdictions and the current location of probate records

Jeremy Gibson, *Probate jurisdictions: where to look for wills* (fourth edition, Federation of Family History Societies, 1994).

The latest edition of this booklet is the most up-to-date guide to the whereabouts of wills.

The parish maps of individual counties published by the Institute of Heraldic and Genealogical Studies, Northgate, Canterbury, show the areas served by the various local courts.

Information about probate records and their value for research

Anthony J Camp, *Wills and their whereabouts* (fourth edition, London, 1974).

This is a much fuller guide to probate records than the FFHS *Probate jurisdictions* (above) but the information about their whereabouts is out of date.

David E Gardner and Frank Smith, *Genealogical research in England and Wales*, Vol II, pp 22-143 (Bookcraft Publishers Utah, 1959).

Eve McLaughlin, *Wills before 1858* (FFHS, fourth edition, 1992).

Terrick V H Fitzhugh, *The Dictionary of Genealogy* (A & C Black, fourth edition revised by Society of Genealogists, 1994).

Help with reading Latin probate clauses and acts of administration

Eve McLaughlin, *Simple Latin for family historians* (fifth edition, FFHS, 1994).

Eileen Gooder, *Latin for local history, an introduction* (second edition, fourth impression, Longman, 1984).

Elizabeth Simpson, *Latin word-list for family historians* (FFHS, 1985).

Janet Morris, *A Latin glossary for family and local historians* (FFHS, 1989).

Michael Gandy, *A basic approach to Latin for family historians* (FFHS, 1995).

Probate Inventories

John West, *Village records* (Phillimore, 1982). Pages 94-131 give many examples, including pictures and plans of houses constructed from inventories. Note that both his bibliography and his list of printed collections of inventories are in two parts: that for the first edition on pages 93 and 129 respectively, but updated to 1981 on page 197. There is also a glossary of unusual words found in inventories on pages 120 to 125.

R. Milward, *Probate inventories - a glossary of household, farming and trade terms* (Derbyshire Record Society, 3rd edition, 1991).

John Moore (ed), *The goods and chattels of our forefathers* (Phillimore, 1976).

F W Steer, *Farm and cottage inventories* (Phillimore, 1969).

Guides to records in the PRO

Jane Cox, *Never been here before* (PRO Readers' Guide no 4, 1993).

Jane Cox and Timothy Padfield, *Tracing your ancestors in the Public Record Office* (HMSO, 4th edition revised by Amanda Bevan and Andrea Duncan, 1992).

David Shorney, *Protestant Nonconformity and Roman Catholicism: a guide to sources in the Public Record Office* (PRO Readers' Guide no 13, 1996).

History of the PCC and Doctors' Commons

G D Squibb, *Doctors' Commons: A history of the College of advocates and doctors of law* (London, 1977).

Charles Dickens, *Sketches by Boz*, chapter VII.

House of Commons Sessional Papers:

1. Report of the Commissioners for examining into the duties, salaries, and emoluments, of the officers, clerks and ministers, of the several courts of justice, in England, Wales and Berwick-upon-Tweed;- As to the court of Arches of the Lord Archbishop of Canterbury, The Prerogative Court of the same Archbishop, and the Court of Peculiars of the same Archbishop, 1823 (1823 (462) VII. 27).

2. The special and general reports made to His Majesty by the Commissioners appointed to inquire into the practice and jurisdiction of the ecclesiastical courts in England and Wales, 1832 (1831-32 (199) XXIV.1).

3. As 2. but reprinted 1843 (1843 (132) XIX. 289).

General interest

Peter Earle, *The making of the English middle class, business society and family life in London 1660-1730* (Methuen, 1991). Uses PCC wills and gives references.

Index

A

Account 22, 64, 68

Act books
see under Administrations; Probate

Addams, proctor 37, 39

Administrations (admons), *passim*
act books xi, 9-13, 17, 21, 33, 43, 60, 64, 68
definition xi, 7, 68
indexes of 1, 2, 7, 8, 14-16, 19-21, 25, 60, 61, 64
limited administrations 17, 18, 23, 24, 64, 69, 70, 72
renunciations by administrators 65, 71
special administrations 17, 18, 64, 69, 72
with the will annexed 7, 14-16, 29, 68

Affidavits 33, 65, 69, 71
see also Depositions

Allegations 33-35, 37, 65, 68
answers to 35, 65

American wills and administrations 62

Answers *see* Allegations

Antigua, tobacco grown in 24

Archdeaconry x
archdeacon's court x, 45
archdeacon's visitation 42

Arches, Court of 75

Army *see* soldiers

Arnold, Richard, will reference of 20

Astley, Philip, will reference of 16

Asylum, keeper 37

B

Bank of England, stock xi, 61

Baptism records, 40

Baptists, 38
Baptist churches 38

Bayly, John, administration of 22

Bellhouse, Jane, will reference of 15

Beneficiaries
date of death 16

relationship to testator 43

Births
date of 38
records 40

Bishops 1
bishop's court *see* Consistory court

Bridport, name of register 16

Brighton, Sussex, resident of, 26

Bristol 2

Burial records 40

C

Calendars 1, 2, 4, 5, 7, 8, 14-17, 19, 21, 68, 69
green calendar, 70

Camp, Anthony, indexes 20, 73

Canterbury
ecclesiastical province x, 11, 55, 70
Prerogative Court *see* Prerogative Court of Canterbury

Capes, clerk of the Surrey seat 9, 10

Captains of ships 24

Causes
contested 65, 69
index of 33
papers 38, 39, 65, 66

Chapman, Elizabeth, litigation on will of 36-39

Cheshire 2

Cheshunt, Herts, resident of 26

Chester 2

Chideock, Dorset, resident of 36, 38

Children, names of 43

Church courts x, xi, 43, 54, 73, 75

Civil War period 25

Clerks of seats 9, 10, 21

Codicils 34, 36, 37, 39, 65, 68

Commissions 22, 34, 36, 65, 66, 68, 69

Commonwealth period (Interregnum) 25, 48

Consistory court x

Corscombe, Dorset *see* Toller Whelme

Courts x, xi, 43, 54, 73, 75
see also under particular courts and types

Women
    administrations of 9, 11, 12, 13, 15, 16
    administratrix 15, 68
    coverture 69
    estates of 24
    executrix 15, 69
    former surnames 14
    testatrix 36-40, 42, 72
    wills of 5, 7, 15, 16, 23, 24, 26, 28-31
    see also Widows

Y

York
    ecclesiastical province x, 55, 56
    Prerogative Court x